AMERICA
AND THE
MULTINATIONAL
CORPORATION

The History of
a Troubled Partnership

JOHN J. REARDON

HD
2785
.R43
1992

PRAEGER

Westport, Connecticut
London

Library of Congress Cataloging-in-Publication Data

Reardon, John J. (John Joseph).
  America and the multinational corporation : the history of a
troubled partnership / John J. Reardon.
    p.   cm.
  Includes bibliographical references and index.
  ISBN 0-275-93918-9 (alk. paper)
    1. International business enterprises—United States—History.
I. Title.
HD2785.R43   1992
338.8'8973—dc20   92-12211

British Library Cataloguing in Publication Data is available.

Library of Congress Catalog Card Number: 92-12211
ISBN: 0-275-93918-9

First published in 1992

Praeger Publishers, 88 Post Road West, Westport, CT 06881
An imprint of Greenwood Publishing Group, Inc.

Printed in the United States of America

∞™

The paper used in this book complies with the Permanent
Paper Standard issued by the National Information Standards
Organization (Z39.48—1984).

10 9 8 7 6 5 4 3 2 1

CONTENTS

PREFACE

The two parties that make up the partnership in this history have been analyzed often and variously by the disciplines concerned with this aspect of America's past. Americans tend to perpetually scrutinize their government not only in terms of how it works, but also in terms of how well it works. Does it dominate, control or win in its quest to serve the nation's interests, or is it subordinate to some other force? The second party in this partnership, the multinational corporation, is a more illusive entity, even less susceptible to neat definition as to form and substance. Since World War II, no comparable economic organization has generated such a vast literature of both praise and condemnation in such a short period of time. And almost always it is assessed in terms of its impact on the United States and on the other countries in which it flourished. It is not an exaggeration to say that since World War II the study of business-government relations in America has become a growth industry in the academic community because this country's perceived historic economic scoundrel, the corporation, acquired a new dimension—a multinational dimension.

What follows is an attempt to reconstruct the ever-changing post-war relationship between the American multinational corporation and the Federal government. It is a record of continuous adjustment on the part of both parties as each side navigated the uncharted waters of this unconventional partnership. What makes it so relevant historically is that while the Federal government was adjusting to its postwar global responsibilities, corporate America in its multinational dimension was taking on new roles: as the dynamic advocate of both the free enterprise system and a pragmatic American idealism, as the architect of a global economy, and, ultimately, as a rather shameful example of how this mid-century quest for market dominance in the global arena almost destroyed the ethical credibility of all corporations in America.

Of necessity, much of this record has to be reconstructed from what are collectively called public documents, in this case not only the formal or official records of the executive and legislative branches of government, but, more specifically, what these branches collected by way of oral testimony or written presentations from executives in the corporate community, spokesmen for the labor unions, and designated representatives of the various supportive or critical interest groups that attempted to get their views before the numerous investigative, regulatory, and policy-making agencies of the Federal government. Such material has an inevitable bias. It normally is a fairly visible bias that, hopefully, has been appropriately discounted in the construction of this narrative.

No serious examination of this subject could, however, be undertaken without using the vast resources of the Baker Library of the Harvard Graduate School of Business Administration and the brilliantly eclectic holdings of the Littauer Library of the John F. Kennedy School of Government. Beyond this I am indebted to the libraries of Brown University, the Government Documents division of Northwestern University and, of course, the library resources of my own University and, closer to my home, to the generous staff of the Lake Forest College library.

And last, but not least, the deferential and unobtrusive "management style" of Jim Dunton, Praeger's Editor-in-Chief, has to be acknowledged—it most certainly spurred the completion of this manuscript.

INTRODUCTION

THE MULTINATIONALIZATION OF CORPORATE AMERICA[1]

Although language is always in a state of flux, the term "multinational corporation" is comparatively recent and apparently American in origin. The concept, however, has its roots in the joint stock companies of the 16th and 17th centuries. These famous state-chartered companies were multinationals, at least to the extent that they represented a business organization with economic goals projected on an international stage. They were also considered instruments of the national state, serving what are now characterized as the geopolitical needs of their "home" countries.

The corporate form, which became the organizational refinement of the joint stock company, acquired its credentials during the age of industrial capitalism. It was an instrument for accumulating and focusing the financial resources of numerous investors on a specific economic venture with the intent of generating a profit for both the corporation and its shareholders. The fact that it acquired its charter from the government in whose political jurisdiction it resided inevitably gave it a special relationship with that government, which in the United States was usually one of the states rather than the Federal government. If there was a visible multinational dimension to business during the early 19th century, it was in the trading and shipping sectors of the economy, where advances in marine technology invited an easy and natural involvement in transoceanic trade.

In the fifty-odd years between the end of the Civil War and America's entry into World War I the United States had no significant benchmarks in the deliberate multinationalization of corporate America. The most obvious explanation was economic self-sufficiency. As a nation, Americans believed themselves to be blessed with an abundance of everything needed to continue the growth they had come to take for granted. And, with the exception of J. P. Morgan & Co. and a few other American-based banking firms, America's business community knew virtually nothing about the only major multinational corporations of the late 19th century, i.e., the merchant banking houses of Europe with their international approach to agency services in finance and/or investment, and their routine processing of bills of exchange to facilitate a substantial growth in foreign transactions in the major capital markets of Europe.

All that changed in the 20th century, most noticeably during World War I, when America's ideological isolationism underwent a dramatic change. Europe's problems became the touchstone of America's economic as well as its political/diplomatic awakening. As a part of its exposure to the outside world, America learned about foreign business practices and how foreign corporations responded to the economic and political dislocations that resulted from a major continental war. Corporate America suddenly understood and appreciated that the United States and its economy by contrast had been virtually untouched by world events.

World War I also gave the American business community a different perspective, and for a select few, a different agenda. If the war did not document the finite nature of America's natural resources, it at least pushed the larger oil, copper, nitrates, rubber, and aluminum companies into making irreversible commitments to foreign investments to ensure their companies' futures. Not only did this set these companies apart from the business practices of most of corporate America, but it also involved significant political and economic risks. Yet, it must be noted, these foreign investments necessitated no fundamental adjustment in terms of a company's management style. Seldom comfortable with the foreign or remote aspects of their corporate structure, these companies took for granted that all their foreign investments should be under the direct control of American executives at the so-called "home" office. During these years, the foreign investment practices in the primary products sector, even when they only involved two or three unavoidable foreign subsidiaries on the CEO's global map, were never an instinctive response to providing for an adequate reserve of the natural resource essential to their survival.

Foreign expansion in the consumer-driven companies such as General Motors, Goodyear, General Electric, and Du Pont was less urgent and therefore less aggressive.[2] Following on the heels of the consumer-driven companies was the inevitable expansion in the service-oriented companies such as those opening American hotels in London or Paris to cater to American businessmen and tourists. All these foreign ventures had the geographic spread to qualify as "multinational corporations" yet, in terms of corporate management and finances, they were really American companies with "subordinate" foreign branches that acquired their justification because they served some specific objective. Unlike companies dependent on a particular natural resource such as oil or copper, the future of these companies did not pivot on the success or failure of their foreign subsidiaries. They were considered valuable in terms of enhancing corporate profits, but they were not the item on the company's balance sheet that was likely to give the corporation an advantage over its domestic competitors. The company's most promising managerial talent was never permanently assigned to the foreign branch office, and no corporate lobbyist came to Washington to argue for a lower corporate tax rate on the income earned from these foreign subsidiaries. More to the point, when the economy collapsed in October, 1929, with the Great Depression, these subsidiaries seldom figured prominently in the company's survival or recovery strategies.

This Depression virtually destroyed the foreign operations of most American firms: only the strongest sought to maintain an economic toehold, a visible presence in countries where the eventual benefits were presumed to outweigh the current losses. Even the major investment and merchant banking firms, the only truly international enterprises outside the primary products sector, were severely hurt, reduced to sheltering as best they could the dwindling reserves of their oldest clients. These developments signaled the demise of virtually all international business and finance.

As the Depression spread, the larger industrial nations desperately tried to salvage their respective economies and to bring some order into the monetary systems of the world. Both American and European corporate executives soon discovered that the various international economic conferences of the '30s were between governments, not business leaders, and that they did not figure prominently in the defensive measures of these governments as these nations addressed the global economic collapse of the Depression years.

The political developments that contributed to the emergence of the modern totalitarian state, followed almost inevitably by an arms race in the late '30s, served as the ultimate vindication of America's instinctive isolationism. Corporate executives, equally committed to the isolationist point of view, considered the domestic market as the only safe market. Foreign trade was an option if there was a market worthy of the risks, but it was not an area of prime concern.

There were exceptions, of course. The corporations in the primary products sector were the most obvious. They attracted attention because they were aggressive, not only in securing new or additional sources of their product, but also because they were buying into other companies to establish an unassailable market position for the future. More importantly, their significant foreign investments had an irreversible quality, making them multinational corporations in the fullest sense of the term.

While World War II and America's involvement therein halted the limited foreign expansion of the late '30s, this war was to become the seedbed of America's global perspective. Hundreds of young men and a smaller number of young women were introduced to foreign cultures that they would otherwise never have known. For some, the experience merely confirmed their American chauvinism, but for others it meant a wholly different outlook on life. They recognized that once the war ended, their world would be vastly different from the world of their parents. Of necessity, World War II gave America an international and, in some cases, a cosmopolitan outlook, thereby defining the climate, if not the agenda, for corporate America in the postwar world.

Initially this meant very little in terms of America's principal prewar markets in Europe, which had been virtually destroyed as a result of the damages inflicted on their economies and infrastructure by several years of conflict. As a result, virtually the only international corporations in the late '40s and early '50s that were truly multinational were in the primary products sector. Real and anticipated shortages caused these corporations to make massive commitments to investments in the Middle East, Latin America, Africa, and Canada. Some even went so far as to rebuild their prewar processing or distribution facilities in Europe. There was also a limited expansion of American corporations into Latin America as the labor-intensive industries established assembly facilities in countries with depressed economies and an ample supply of cheap unskilled labor. Much of this latter form of multinationalization, however, involved a negative assessment of the American labor movement and its postwar aggressiveness, rather than a positive commitment to conduct business on a multinational scale.

The first real impetus to the multinationalization process in the industrial and service sectors developed during the late '50s. As a result of America's massive postwar aid to assist war-ravaged countries, the international economy had recovered sooner than expected and was sufficient to create a favorable economic climate for corporate expansion. Although the political climate was somewhat destabilized by Cold War tensions, one dimension of this worrisome East-West confrontation was a clear delineation of where the free enterprise system and democratically-oriented governments prevailed and where they did not. Equally important were the major advances that had taken place in transportation and communication as a result of the technological advances made during the war. The adoption of the jet engine by commercial aviation shortened travel times and substantial advances in telecommunication permitted corporate executives to talk with business associates in London or Tokyo as readily as they talked to someone in the next office, lessening the traditional concern of American executives about the administrative problems intrinsic to world-wide operations.

At the managerial level, the introduction of the computer and the advent of business machine accounting provided the necessary tools for assessing what the MBA programs were calling "economies of scale," i.e., a corporation's ability to determine at what point the expansion of one's production capacities produced diseconomies, thus reducing a company's profits. Technical efficiency by a professional management corps distrustful of 19th century-style entrepreneurial risk-taking ensured the development of a decision-making process employing the most advanced theories of management science.

As a result of World War II, corporate America knew how to manage a large firm efficiently, generating sufficient profits to satisfy its stockholders. What remained to be accomplished was recognizing the presence of those global economic incentives that made multinationalization desirable. Europe's rapid economic recovery was the most obvious incentive; it signaled the revival of America's single most important market.[3]

Yet, before corporate America seriously considered moving into Europe, Europe began to take on a different character, seeking economic and political leverage against the uncertainties of the postwar world by establishing "communities."[4] The Organization for European Economic Cooperation, created in 1948 as a functional organization to facilitate the reconstruction efforts of European countries receiving Marshall Plan aid, represented a move in the direction of economic federalism. One year later, the Council of Europe brought together European intellectuals and statesmen with an interest in political federalism. These initial steps in the direction of solving Europe's problems through a community approach led to the formation of the Benelux Economic Union in 1948, the European Coal and Steel Community in 1951, and the European Defense Community (EDC) in 1952. The refusal of the French Assembly to support the EDC and the fundamental differences between England and France over the appropriate method for moving toward European federalism sparked a new initiative that would decisively alter the economic map of Europe.

After the French Assembly rejected the EDC Treaty, the Benelux countries urged that instead of a political union, the countries should work for an economic union. What was envisioned was basically a more elaborate and cohesive customs union than had been created by the three-country Benelux Economic Union.[5] The idea took hold and after several years of frequently counterproductive negotiations, France, West Germany, Italy, the Netherlands, Belgium, and Luxembourg signed the Treaty of Rome in March of 1957, creating the European Economic Community (EEC).

Western Europe was now divided into two trade blocks, the Community (the EEC or Common Market) and the major trading nations outside of it—Britain, Norway, Sweden, Denmark, Austria, Switzerland, and Portugal, which, in turn, ultimately formed the European Free Trade Area (EFTA). To the extent that either or both of these customs unions discriminated against American companies with markets in Europe or competed with American companies on the world market, they posed potentially serious problems for corporate America. To the extent that the EEC, the more aggressive of the two, achieved selective or complete economic integration, it forced America's corporations to devise a different structure for their

European investments. Unlike any other single force, the Common Market stimulated multinationalization in America's manufacturing and service enterprises. Add to that the EEC's provisions for the free movement of labor and capital within the Common Market and the beginnings of discussions on the merger of member-countries' economic policies in taxation, transportation, and agriculture; and corporate America faced a formidable challenge.

Theoretically at least, the multinationalization process was merely a geographical extension of corporate growth. More specifically, it represented an effort to devise a permanent network of controls over a corporation's own international activities. The tools, technology, and management theory were in place, all that was needed was a force that made corporate inaction a guaranteed formula for failure in a promising international market. That force was the formation of the EEC or Common Market or, on a more basic level, any agreement that sought to integrate the economies of several countries to the exclusion of those enterprises that were not a part of these economic communities.

By the mid-'50s, Europe again had the elemental requirements for American investments, i.e., responsible governments no longer threatened by indigenous Communist parties, expanding economies with the uncertainties of postwar recovery generally behind them, relatively stable currencies, internationally recognized central banks, and, most important of all, viable markets. When Europe moved beyond this to the initial manifestations of economic federalism (and possibly political federalism) to the exclusion of others, it forced all American corporations that were economically oriented toward Europe to become fully integrated corporate enterprises *within* the EEC. They did what corporations that functioned in the primary products sector had been doing for years to protect their source of supply: they made a major commitment to permanent corporate facilities in one or more foreign countries—they became multinational corporations.

Fascination with the gradualist formula employed by the EEC to neutralize nationalism or the counterproductive tendencies evident in the Anglo-French rivalry over how economic federalism should be maintained in Europe should not obscure the fact that the Common Market was in fact a viable customs union. Any geographically contiguous area of the globe could establish such a union that, by its very nature, would be discriminatory since it was formed to enhance and protect the economies of its signatories.[6] On a practical level, corporate multinationalization was a way of getting inside a customs union, establishing fully integrated self-managing corporations that could benefit from the preferential treatment accorded to the business enterprises functioning in the member nations. On a more theoretical level, American corporate multinationalization in the late '50s and beyond was the private sector's recognition of the internationalization of the economy, an institutional or structural manifestation of growing global interdependence. Corporate America might have led the way and been the most visible practitioner of multinationalization during these years, but it was a phenomenon that would never be uniquely American.

GOVERNMENT AS PARTNER

Over the years the Federal government's relationship with corporate America has become a mixture of controls and supports, easy to track but difficult to reconcile. The conflicting initiatives that prevailed throughout much of the late 19th and early 20th centuries had a common ingredient. Each sought to address problems or issues that were essentially domestic. The inconsistencies were usually attributed to the multiplicity of policy-making agencies and their different perspectives as to the place and function of the corporation in American society. It also must be recognized that many of the inconsistencies were traceable to the activities of special interest groups pushing and pulling on the policy-making process.

However, during World War II and more particularly after 1945, business-government relations began to acquire another dimension, a kind of partnership that was an outgrowth of corporate America's production record in World War II. Its wartime accomplishments obviously muted much of the criticism of the prewar years, criticism that was further muted by the business community's hostility to all shades of liberal thought during the Red Scare and the politics of anticommunism in the immediate postwar period. Quite simply, the ideological environment in which corporate America functioned had changed. Respected liberal reformers of the '30s were now suspected of being communist sympathizers, and labor unions, previously above criticism, were now said to be corrupt, greedy, and so disruptive of the surging postwar economy that congressional scrutiny and strong antilabor legislation was deemed essential.[7] Instead of an instinctive readiness to believe anything reprehensible about the machinations of big business, corporate bashing gradually became more selective and more precise. Even the conglomerate phenomenon of the '60s invited more economic analysis of its implications than ideological denunciation of its dangers. At the very least, being pro-big business in the immediate postwar years was probably less risky than it had been at any time since the turn of the century. Thus the partnership concept took root in a fairly positive political climate, the Cold War supplying a geopolitical imperative to this linkage.

The initial partnership that developed during World War II had been at the urging of the Federal government, with corporate America being the willing recipient of generous government contracts that reflected the urgency and massiveness of our wartime needs. But the end of the war did not signal the end of the partnership. In 1944, as the European conflict was drawing to a close, Dean Acheson, the Assistant Secretary of State, noted the complementary nature of public and private foreign lending and urged that encouragement of private investment abroad be incorporated into U.S. postwar economic policy.[8] The investment guarantee provisions of the Economic Cooperation Act of 1948 implementing the Marshall Plan for the reconstruction of war-torn Europe supported this idea, and when the concept became an essential component of Truman's Point IV program, it acquired an even greater visibility.[9] The idea of the Federal government offering investment guarantees to those corporations that expanded into the less-developed regions of the world inevitably suggested a long-term partnership. Under the administration's proposal, investment guarantees were to include any "risks peculiar to such investments," seemingly a blanket form of protection. While this feature of Truman's Point IV program never received congressional funding, it did generate a thorough debate as to the appropriate role of the Federal government in promoting private foreign investments in high-risk areas.[10]

The investment guarantee concept was reactivated in 1951 with the establishment of the Mutual Security Agency, which, while authorized to promote private foreign investments, was primarily concerned with the economic stability and military security of those areas of the world presumed to be threatened by Communist expansion. The numerous administrative changes of the next few years suggested an unfocused mandate in the executive branch and no broad-based support within the legislative branch for a vigorous investment guarantee program. Yet it was during these years that the technical aspects of an investment guarantee program came under closer scrutiny.

There was the obvious question of giving the program an economic and geographical focus (developed, less-developed, underdeveloped, and/or undeveloped areas of the world) and a further concern as to the scope of its insurance provisions. Specifically, should it protect corporate investments against losses resulting from all the hazards of foreign investments (war, revolution, insurrection, expropriation, and the nonconvertibility of a foreign currency) or merely expropriation?[11] In the final analysis what this question addressed was the attractiveness of the program to corporate America and how it could be made more useful to those firms contemplating foreign expansion.

The investment guarantee program acquired a higher profile in 1955 when the program and its professional staff were transferred to the International Cooperation Administration, a semiautonomous agency within the State Department.[12] The Mutual Security Act of 1956 increased the effectiveness of the program even further and extended its authority to issue investment guarantees through the year 1967. In November, 1961, when the International Cooperation Administration was dissolved, its functions were absorbed by the Agency for International Development (AID), also a part of the State Department.[13]

Aside from the investment guarantee program, the Federal government also made direct loans to corporate America to promote specific foreign investments. The Export-Import Bank of Washington (Eximbank) was authorized to make loans to American firms seeking to establish foreign branches or manufacturing facilities. In virtually every case the loans were in support of projects that could not be financed through American capital markets because they represented investments in countries that private U.S. banks deemed too risky for their funds.[14]

A further source of loan money was provided in 1957 by the Cooley Amendment to the Agricultural, Trade, Development, and Assistance Act that had been passed in 1954. The amendment authorized the use of foreign currencies that had been received in payment for the sale of American surplus agricultural products as loans to corporations "operating" in the countries where the funds were collected.[15] In principle at least, both of these loan programs reflected the Federal government's continuing efforts to develop a partnership with a generally reluctant corporate America.

All that began to change in 1959–1960. A loosely defined notion of partnership took on new meaning for corporate America after Cuba's Fidel Castro expropriated American businesses worth $1.375 billion, followed almost immediately by the seizure of the ESSO and Texaco refineries on the Island because these companies refused to process Russian crude oil.[16] It should be understood that long before Castro, Cuba had become a showcase of the best and worst of American corporate multinationalization. Suddenly it became something more, a dramatic illustration of a host government's hostility to America's economic penetration of Latin America.

Traditionally, the popular response to perceived threats to American interests in Latin America had been to "send in the Marines"—or at least threaten to do so. However, the Bay of Pigs fiasco suggested that the government had to develop radically different methods of protecting American corporate interests. And this seemed to be true for all areas of the world where national aspirations clashed with American economic penetration.

The State Department, responding to a growing uncertainty both in and out of government as to the efficacy of military solutions to specific economic problems, began to formulate policy from a different perspective. If American security or vital natural resources were not at stake (and that was an important "if"), perhaps the best way to protect American foreign investments was to avoid exacerbating political tensions. Initially this approach involved "isolating Castroism" on the theory that the spread of Communism in Latin America was more detrimental to American interests in that region than the increasingly frequent instances of military dictatorships. But as American economic interests, and especially American corporations, began to expand around the globe, more and more attention was given to smoothing the political climate for these corporations. The administrations of Eisenhower, Kennedy, Johnson, and Nixon all seemed to subscribe to an assuasive approach wherever there was a heavy concentration of American business interests in a volatile political climate. Valid or not, it was perceived that being a silent partner was a more effective form of support than being an aggressive advocate.

Practically speaking, this involved urging multinational corporations to make peace with the government in power. Where there appeared to be a clash of personalities or inherent managerial hostility toward the government or people in power in the host country, the government advised the multinational corporation to replace its current executives with a new management team from the United

States. And if national pride created particular tensions, the government suggested that the multinational corporation bring more of the
host country's recognized and respected business leaders into their
organization at the managerial level. In some cases the advice focused
not on the composition of the companies' corporate management,
but on the political and economic implications of volatile racial
conflict such as was true in Rhodesia and South Africa. This is not to
say that political representation by the embassy personnel on the
scene or by the State Department had been abandoned. Quite the
contrary, multinational corporations and global interdependence
made the day-to-day workings of American diplomacy exceedingly
complex and filled with inevitable inconsistencies.

Furthermore, there was a continuous dialogue between Congress
and the Treasury Department over the technical provisions of the
U.S. tax codes with respect to the foreign income of American
multinational corporations. At issue was whether the amount a
corporation paid in taxes to a foreign government on income earned
in that country should be treated as "deductions" or "credits" when
determining the tax liability of the corporation to its own government.
And there was also the question of whether corporate income from
foreign subsidiaries was taxable during the calendar year it was
earned or whether it should not be taxed until it was "repatriated"
back to the United States as profits. This debate over "deductions"
versus "credits", as well as the question of taxing corporate profits
before or after they were brought back into the United States, was in
fact a debate over how the Federal government should or should not
use its tax laws to assist the multinational corporation. Given America's
historic hostility toward double taxation, it was obvious that there
would be some level of credits on the taxes paid to foreign governments.
Whatever was done beyond that to protect corporate profits represented deliberate tax benefits, frequently justified or explained with
the argument that the multinational corporation was directly or
indirectly serving American foreign policy interests.[17] A less visible
part of the tax incentives approach to enhancing the partnership was
the State Department's efforts to negotiate agreements or treaties
harmonizing the tax laws between the United States and those
foreign governments having significant American corporate investments. When sizeable investments were involved, the tax harmonization process usually took on a greater urgency.

There was also a modest partnership component in the tortured
history of America's postwar tariff policy insofar as the multinational

corporation was concerned. Much of it remained buried in a broader debate over the nature and scope of our reciprocal trade policy. Continued wrangling over the kinds of limits that should be placed on the negotiating authority of the Executive in determining tariff rates, on whether there should be a "peril point" provision and/or an "escape clause"[18] in each of the trade extension bills considered by Congress, all took precedence over reconciling our tariff policy with the growing reality of the multinationalization of corporate America.

The only visible form of accommodation with corporate multinationalization in our postwar tariff policy was the adjustment in the tariff rates for American multinational corporations importing items manufactured by their subsidiaries back into the United States for their own exclusive use. In most cases the adjustment involved importing the item tariff-free. Since a corporation's decision to establish a foreign subsidiary primarily for the purpose of supplying a labor-intensive item for the parent company reflected a refusal to accept the higher labor costs inherent in the U.S. domestic economy, these "exceptions" were not something that a multinational corporation cared to publicize. It really involved quiet lobbying in Congress rather than openly exploiting the partnership aspects of government-business relations. Concessions to the multinational corporation in this respect were more than the traditional domestically-oriented supports usually associated with each successive tariff revision. These concessions were perceived to be the most explicitly antilabor aspect of the partnership with the multinational corporation.

The ultimate institutional manifestation of the government's partnership with the multinational corporation was the Overseas Private Investment Corporation (OPIC), established in December of 1969.[19] Within a matter of two or three years, it was viewed by both critics and supporters as the "principle instrumentality" of the Federal government in stimulating private investment in developing countries.[20] OPIC operated on a self-sustaining basis as a semiautonomous government corporation, providing investment insurance, investment guarantees, research assistance, and direct loans to American corporations committed to foreign investments—offered with only minimal technical restrictions and even less direct oversight.[21] Its scope made it a ready target of those who had little sympathy for the American multinational corporation and even less for the government's role in supporting its expansion. When its operations came under congressional scrutiny in the early '70s, it was discovered that OPIC, required by law to conduct its operations with due regard for the "principles of risk management" like any other insurance company, had responded to this legislative directive by shifting away from its original mission of supporting "high-risk economic development projects" in Third World countries and instead became identified with essentially low-risk projects in economically developed countries.[22] OPIC had become a profit-oriented government insurance company and, by the late '70s, a highly profitable institutional manifestation of the partnership aspect of foreign investment guarantees.[23]

In the final analysis, the Federal government's efforts to promote direct foreign investments to further its foreign policy objectives pivoted largely on some form of investment guarantees, first in Europe and then in less-developed or underdeveloped regions of the world. Because the government had only limited means of protecting these investments, it tried to anticipate problems by negotiating bilateral or multilateral treaties that it then cited as evidence that a given country had a favorable investment climate for American businesses.[24]

But the corporation, believing that a foreign government bent on harassment will in fact harass—regardless of what the American government said or did—assessed the situation somewhat differently. While never ignoring what the Federal government provided by way of assistance, it made its own assessment of a country's political and economic maturity and the adequacy of that country's existing infrastructure before committing corporate resources to a foreign operation.

Regardless of the number and variety of the procedures used, the Federal government's ability to forge a partnership with the American multinational corporation was usually limited by the multinational's own perception of the economic viability of each foreign investment opportunity.

NOTES

1. This section is primarily concerned with the process that prompted corporate America to acquire a predominantly multinational dimension after 1950—to have direct foreign investments with book values of $11.8 billion in 1950, $32.0 billion in 1960, $78.1 billion in 1970, and $107.3 billion in 1973. (U.S. Congress, Senate, Committee on Finance, *Implications of Multinational Firms for World Trade and Investment and for U.S. Trade and Labor* [Washington: G.P.O., 1973], p. 72 and U.S. Department of Commerce, *Survey of Current Business* [Aug. 1974], part II, pp. 18–19.)

2. Although it is dangerous to generalize, this form of foreign expansion was essentially in assembly or distribution plants and sales offices for market penetration, or expansion for access to patents or some specific technology.

3. The conventional generic breakdown of business enterprise is extractive or primary product, manufacturing, and service-oriented businesses. Extractive or primary product enterprises became multinational when the domestic source of their product was judged insufficient to satisfy future demand or, as was true with rubber, nonexistent in the 48 contiguous states. Manufacturing and service enterprises became multinational when market forces dictated the development of a business structure more elaborate than branch offices or subordinate one-function subsidiaries. In general, therefore, the manufacturing and service enterprises were more interested in developed than underdeveloped areas. Since Europe was the first familiar developed area to recover after World War II, it had a particular significance in the multinationalization process in so far as corporate America was concerned.

The extractive or primary products enterprises usually ignored the distinction between developed and underdeveloped. They were concerned with securing an adequate supply of a raw material irrespective of the level of economic development in the country where the product was located.

4. The literature on this subject is enormous. A good general study written from the perspective of the late '70s is Dennis Swann, *The Economics of the Common Market,* 4th ed. (London: Penguin Books, 1978). See also Robert C. Mowat, *Creating the European Community* (New York: Barnes & Noble Books, 1973).

5. Belgium, Luxembourg, and the Netherlands.

6. Custom unions were created in Latin America, the Latin American Free Trade Association; Central America, the Central American Common Market; and Africa, the Organization of African Unity. The last named organization was, of course, more than a dedicated customs union.

7. The Taft-Hartley Act, an explicitly anti-union measure, was passed over a presidential veto on June 23, 1947. Starting in January, 1957, the McClellan Committee began an investigation of union affairs, its disclosures generating the Landrum-Griffin Act of 1959, the second major piece of legislation directed against labor unions.

8. Marina von Neumann Whitman, *Government Risk-Sharing in Foreign Investment* (Princeton: Princeton University Press, 1965), p. 19.

9. See chapter 3.

10. *Congressional Quarterly Almanac 1949,* pp. 392–400, quote on p. 392 (henceforth cited as *CQA*).

11. Whitman, *Government Risk-Sharing in Foreign Investment,* pp. 79–81.

12. Ibid., p. 80.

13. Ibid., p. 87. It was this legislation that also allowed the Development Loan Fund to expire, its functions also absorbed by AID.

14. Ibid., pp. 209–254. Private banks, lured by big profits, began to assume many of these risks in the '70s and '80s.

15. Edmund Pendleton, Jr., "Foreign Currency Loans to Private Business," *The Commercial and Financial Chronicle,* March 20, 1958.

16. Mira Wilkins, *The Maturing of Multinational Enterprise: American Business*

Abroad from 1914 to 1970 (Cambridge: Harvard Universit; Press, 1974), pp. 351, 355, 361n.

It should be noted that few firms in Cuba had taken advantage of the investment guarantee options available to them prior to Castro's seizure of power. As a result their losses were substantial.

17. The Federal government usually responded negatively to the efforts of several of the states to tax the gross profits of multinational corporations head-quartered in their states. It supported the corporate position that a state government only had the right to tax the profits earned on company operations within the state.

18. A "peril point" is the minimal point below which a tariff cut would hurt a domestic industry. The Tariff Commission would determine the point rather than have it defined in the law itself. An "escape clause" is any mechanism by which a tariff rate might be raised to provide relief to a domestic industry that had been hurt by imports stemming from tariff cuts. Both concepts were reflective of a domestic focus in the writing of tariff legislation.

19. *CQA, 1969*, pp. 434–437.

20. U.S. Congress, House, Committee on Foreign Affairs, Study prepared for ... by Congressional Research Service, *The Overseas Private Investment Corporation: A Critical Analysis, September 4, 1973* (Washington: G.P.O., 1973), p. v.

21. Ibid.

22. Ibid., quote on p. 1.

23. Clyde H. Farnsworth, "A Spotlight on Obscure Agency," *New York Times*, February 19, 1990, pp. C1 and C3.

24. As Marina von Neumann Whitman observed in 1965:

The growth of public lending and guarantying institutions, along with the proliferation of other forms of governmental encouragement of international capital flows, is rapidly forcing us [specialists in international political economy] to develop new definitions of private foreign investments.... Instead of a neat juxtaposition of private *versus* public investment, we are faced with a seemingly unbroken continuum: moving from private investment without government assistance at all, through the use of government information services, tax relief, limited guaranties (insurance), joint public-private lending, and total repayment guaranties to loans made entirely from public funds. (Whitman, *Government Risk-Sharing in Foreign Investment*, p. 66.)

1 THE POLITICAL CONTEXT: 1890–1939

The corporate form of business organization was an inevitable institution in most industrialized societies regardless of the ideological persuasion of the country in which it developed. However, in the United States, the free enterprise system and democratic spirit offered a particularly fertile ground for its vigorous growth. Thus, at least since the middle of the 19th century, corporations have held a prominent position in American society, growing in influence as the number, size, and diversity of corporate enterprises increased.

The American corporation had its roots in the late 18th and early 19th centuries, but as an economic institution it did not acquire credentials or critics until the last quarter of the 19th century. Credentials came first; the manner in which it coordinated economic resources and human talent on any profit-oriented venture could not be equalled. It was viewed as a mechanism that seemed able to do almost anything, becoming the hallmark of American economic vitality in the post–Civil War years. And the fact that England's industrial revolution, which predated America's by nearly a century, made little use of the corporate form of business during the 18th and early 19th centuries only served to make it the preeminent contribution of America to western industrialization.

Demonstrating its utility first in canal building, mining, and railroading, and then in the oil industry, the corporation under the masterful and sometimes unscrupulous guidance of America's colorful entrepreneurs, quickly proved its worth. As a result, Americans in the 19th century initially enshrined it as one of the institutions that made the country great. But "power to do" inevitably led to "power over," and corporations soon became a dubious blessing. Those who questioned the conceptual magnificence of the corporation could be dismissed as impulsive critics of bigness, but those who asked embarrassing questions about the corporation's "power over" could not be dismissed simply as malcontents. The American dream was to be the biggest and the best, to have the most impressive statistics in terms of economic growth and power, but not at the expense of freedom. "Power over" was always an uncomfortable accommodation in the political sphere, an inevitable characteristic of government even in a democratic society; "power over" in economic terms suggested self-serving entrepreneurs exploiting others for their own gain.

Criticism of the corporation in the late 19th century, however, was essentially criticism of size and power rather than structure. Terms like "monopoly," "trust," and "political influence" were the standard labels of disapproval, but the essential complaint behind all of them was bigness. John D. Rockefeller's Standard Oil Company had acquired a "virtual monopoly" of the oil industry, and he and his obedient lieutenants were manipulating not only the market and certain railroads, but even state legislatures in their quest for power. That practice clashed with one of America's most cherished precepts, the proposition that, in a democratic society, the people's representatives, functioning through the legislative process, were the ones who made the rules.[1]

Initial attempts to deprive the large corporations of their power emerged out of the fears and hostility of the farmer, the small businessman, and the laborer. Efforts were made at state regulation, followed within a few years by Federal laws. Directed against the railroads, the Interstate Commerce Act of 1887 was the first piece of Federal regulatory legislation passed by Congress; it was followed by the Sherman Antitrust Act of 1890, which was aimed at curbing the predatory practices of the big corporations. The vagueness of both laws and the common law roots of the latter made both pieces of legislation essentially ineffectual. But a different perspective on business-government relations had been introduced, the device of a permanent regulatory commission and the concept of antitrust had been institutionalized, discarding for all time the notion that laissez-faire competition was the central regulatory mechanism of the American economy.

Yet this regulation, or pseudo-regulation, was but one dimension of a multifaceted association between business and government that extended back to the Washington administration. Beginning with Secretary of the Treasury Alexander Hamilton's proposal for a Bank of the United States and his meticulous Report on Manufacturing, which clearly envisioned a major role for government in America's economic development, some form of mutual cooperation was presumed. Over the years, the supportive role of government was reflected in direct subsidization of certain economic activities—tariffs for those who argued that they needed protection from the dynamics of a more advanced European economy, and liberal land grants to railroads in the West to help finance their construction. Aside from tariffs, a similar list of "supports" could be compiled between many states and the major economic enterprises operating within their borders. With some obvious exceptions, most of these associations were between business and the legislative branch of government, with the executive and the judiciary branches playing a passively supportive role. The birth of a pseudo-regulatory climate in the final decades of the 19th century, while not a repudiation of the neomercantilism of earlier decades, did signal an abandonment of all of the vestiges of classic laissez-faire economic policy.[2]

The response of big business to the linkage of neomercantilism with regulation was two-fold. In the case of the railroads and the Interstate Commerce Commission, the technique was to capture the agency that was supposed to do the regulating, and in the case of the Sherman Antitrust Act, the response of the corporate community was to exploit the vagueness of the act and the economic conservatism of the Federal judiciary to narrow the meaning and application of the law. This suggests that corporate America was insidious, neutralizing the regulatory intent of the Populist-minded reformers if not the politically-sensitive lawmakers who fashioned these laws. It also suggests that the business community was adept at more than conventional lobbying techniques. The century ended with railroad regulation and the antitrust movement having only symbolic significance, while the schedules in the McKinley tariff of 1890 and the Dingley tariff of 1897 signaled that business and government were anything but bitter enemies.[3]

Corporate America found the regulatory climate of the first decade-and-a-half of the 20th century set by a nebulous concept known as Progressivism, which manifested itself under such broad labels as social justice, political reform, social welfare, and public control. To the extent that one or more of these terms meant government regulation or explicitly disallowing certain business practices, they met with considerable opposition in the business community and generated ideological distrust of government at all levels and against all branches except possibly the judiciary.

From the vantage point of the businessman, they came at a time when economic forces in the United States and throughout the world were promoting the development of the large firm. The Morgan group in steel and banking and the Rockefeller alliance of oils, railroads, and banking were only the most visible and dramatic manifestations of this development. More significant and more permanent developments were the initial advances in technology and communication, the emergence of sophisticated techniques in marketing, and the creation of a professional management structure. The economic climate was beginning to generate what, for lack of a better term, was called the "modern" corporation. And it was doing so in a seemingly hostile political climate because Presidents Theodore Roosevelt and William Howard Taft had succeeded in putting the antitrust movement on the front pages of virtually every American newspaper. In 1911, the court-ordered dissolution of the oil and tobacco monopolies proved that the Federal judiciary was responsive to Progressivism's hostility to business combinations in restraint of trade if not against the more basic issue of bigness in business. Wilson's vacillating position vis-à-vis the Clayton Antitrust Act during his first term and his belated acceptance of the Federal Trade Commission bill put the capstone on the antitrust movement until the late 1930s.[4]

The choices the U.S. government had made between 1890 and 1914 with respect to corporate America, however, were far less ominous than the political record might suggest. The courts, particularly the Federal courts, were unwilling to convert the general language of the laws into crusades, and the regulatory apparatus, while initially arousing fear, was far less menacing in fact than it was in theory. Business could freely engage in lobbying or finance the campaigns of sympathetic legislators to foster their point of view.

World War I generated comparatively few permanent changes. The mobilization of industry, never effective until Wilson made Bernard M. Baruch chairman of the War Industries Board, proved to be a short-lived and not always smooth experiment in government-sponsored centralization.[5] It dissolved, like so many wartime agencies, almost as soon as the Armistice was signed in 1918, resulting in the prompt return of the railroads and America's merchant fleet to private ownership and the end of all wartime wage and price controls. For the business community this represented an almost frantic lunge toward "normalcy," the catchword of the postwar era.

In short, with the possible exception of the war years, business had shaped its own environment for at least half a century. And while many Americans remained highly critical of the methods of big business, it was still widely recognized that "no political party standing for severe interference by the state [with the private enterprise system] had ever gained more than a small percentage of the national vote."[6]

In the '20s, three successive Republican administrations fostered an economic climate that was marked more by supports than controls. The supports came in the form of moderate tariff increases, a Federal Trade Commission that fashioned a narrowly focused regulatory climate that business was reluctant to criticize, a virtually dormant judiciary on antitrust matters, and an open support among various government agencies and departments of what was being referred to as intercorporate cooperation. This latter development represented an alternative adopted by business to avoid the cutthroat competition methods of earlier decades. The vestiges of Progressivism, which secured some notable victories in an effort to help the farmer, failed to have a permanent impact on the prevailing economic climate of this era.

And it has to be said that the fundamental shift in the international economic balance of power from Europe to the United States that took place during these years found the business community (the oil companies and banking community excepted) as much under the influence of an isolationist mentality as was the rest of the country. It was only the Departments of State and Commerce that took up the challenges of international economic opportunity, working diligently to protect America's economic interests abroad.[7]

If most of the American business community failed to respond to these changes in the international economic arena, it did not ignore the domestic opportunities presented by three successive Republican administrations committed to an essentially conservative economic policy. Accepting the court's "rule of reason" interpretation of the Sherman Antitrust Act, corporate leaders opted for oligopoly over monopoly and cultivated the appropriate senators and representatives to further their economic priorities. In tariff and tax matters, businessmen followed the standard formula of using trade associations to convey their collective needs or fears.

The predisposition toward business, evident under Wilson as well as Harding, Coolidge, and Hoover, led to the gradual transformation of the regulatory agencies and even the Federal Power Commission into benevolent instruments of business interests. There was opposition, to be sure, as the surprising defeat of a bill to allow the private development of the Muscle Shoals hydroelectric project on the Tennessee River demonstrated. Yet, in general, business and government maintained a kind of arms-length cordiality.

By the end of the '20s, the United States had "stumbled" into a kind of "industrial policy" that involved applying the antitrust laws narrowly and generally enfranchising private utilities under modest regulation. By comparison to Europe, which clearly opted for an expansion of public over private enterprise, the policy represented an essentially modest approach to economic control.[8]

But the panic of 1929 and the subsequent Depression would bring all these patterns into question and put corporate America, in fact, virtually all of business, on the defensive for the first time in American history. The Great Depression profoundly altered the attitude of the business community toward its own invincibility and toward the appropriate role of government in economic affairs. With the possible exception of the Reconstruction Finance Corporation extending financial assistance to banks, life insurance companies, building and loan societies, railroads, and farm loan associations, Hoover's Depression-inspired recovery efforts had no lasting impact on business-government relations.

Yet the ideological convictions of the Hoover administration initiated the first substantive debate between the advocates of laissez-faire economics and the defenders of an American brand of neomercantilism. This debate, though marked by both scornful and justifying rhetoric among political analysts and academicians, should not obscure the fact that Hoover addressed the severe economic realities of the Depression by deliberately forging a consultative link between the business community and the executive branch that each of his successors has accepted as essential to the implementation of his own economic policy. The Great Depression permitted Hoover to do what no previous President had dared to do—to openly and publicly make business leaders partners in the administration's economic recovery policies. Labor leaders and representatives of agriculture were also consulted, but the business and financial communities were given the initial responsibility for absorbing the burdens of the Depression. The fact that they could not or would not do so should not obscure the significance of Hoover's initiatives. Business had been accustomed to using government, specifically Congress; now government, specifically the executive, was using business.[9]

But a storm had broken across America, and Hoover's cautious and hesitant Progressivism, burdened with the baggage of laissez-faire economics, could not stem its tide. With so many victims, a simple holding action was not enough. Franklin Delano Roosevelt, the standard-bearer of the Democratic Party in the presidential election of 1932, was optimism, style, pragmatism, and hope—wrapped in irresistible rhetoric. And the New Deals he proposed were sufficiently vague and flexible to give the corporate community a role in America's economic recovery. They felt the weight of these New Deals, but the New Deals felt their weight as well, and neither business nor government would ever be the same again.

The "first" New Deal has been called an "experiment in compromise,"[10] and to the extent that it was, the business community had to share its influence with other sectors of the American economic community and to operate in the dynamic pluralism that was to be the hallmark of American society for the remainder of the 20th century. If at first businessmen feared and distrusted Roosevelt, their fears were put to rest by his prompt efforts to shore up the nation's banking system. The Emergency Banking Act of March, 1933 involving the administration's commitment to restore and strengthen private ownership in the banking community, signaled, above all else, a determination not to nationalize the engine of the free enterprise system— the nation's banks. The administration's subsequent regulatory legislation of both the banking and securities industries was perceived as being in the tradition of cautious Progressivism, which Hoover had previously sanctioned during his administration.[11] If the business community had a negligible role in the formulation of these supervisory measures, they were not disapproving. The Glass-Steagall Act of June 16, 1933, with its Federal Deposit Insurance Corporation (FDIC) apparatus, and the financial disclosure provisions required under the law creating the Securities and Exchange Commission (SEC), as well as the revamping of the Federal Reserve System, all had the tacit approval of the corporate business community.

The National Recovery Administration (NRA), involving business-government cooperation in drafting fair trade codes, and the

Public Works Administration, a deliberate attempt to stimulate industry through a massive program of public works, further confirmed business' cautious endorsement of Roosevelt. If the National Recovery Administration was considered an experiment in a planned economy, fully justified by the worsening Depression, it also proved that Roosevelt was accepting the principle of self-regulation by the business community as the mechanism most appropriate for this planned economy.

The "first" New Deal gave corporate America a prominent place in the formulation of a Depression-focused economic policy. The corporate community learned to share that role with the representatives of labor and agriculture. Businessmen also learned how important it was to work more closely with the executive branch of government, finding friends and placating enemies among the upper echelon of policy-makers in an expanding government bureaucracy. A strong and pragmatic President and a serious Depression had brought about a shift in focus within the business community, from an historic reliance on the legislative branch to protect business interest, to a willingness to work with the executive branch to salvage the nation's economy.

The so-called "second" New Deal of the mid-'30s was another matter. To the extent that Roosevelt assumed the leadership of a coalition of the victims of the Depression (workers, farmers, the lower middle class, and the unemployed), he seemed to be positioning the "second" New Deal to the ideological left of the "first" New Deal. His annual message to Congress in January, 1935, proposed a different approach, involving a massive relief program that would put all able individuals who were unemployed to work on slum clearance, rural housing, rural electrification, and expanded public works, as well as initiating a Social Security program. His annual message left little doubt that Roosevelt had abandoned business as the prime instrument of recovery. The political-economic coalition that was behind the "second" New Deal was more disturbing to the business community than the substantive aspects of the legislation itself.

Even more alarming was Roosevelt's court reorganization bill of February, 1937, which would allow him to appoint a new judge to the U.S. Supreme Court whenever an incumbent failed to retire after reaching the age of seventy. This effort to deliberately restructure the Supreme Court reflected the freedom Roosevelt presumed he had by virtue of his overwhelming victory in the presidential election of 1936. It was perceived as representing a dangerous expansion of executive power that could not be justified by that victory. This court reorganization effort split the Democratic party, virtually destroying the great coalition of the "second" New Deal. It had to be temporarily revived in 1938 to address the hardships of the so-called Roosevelt recession of 1937–1938, only to disintegrate again a few months later when Roosevelt signaled his intention to once again change the focus of his administration.

The President's call for an investigation of "private power" that had become "stronger than . . . [the] democratic state itself" was perceived as dangerous political rhetoric from a man already considered far too powerful for the office he held. Whether these remarks in April of 1938 and his decision to curb the growing concentration of economic power by initiating an ambitious antitrust campaign are interpreted as the last manifestation of the "second" New Deal or the initial thrust of a "third" New Deal, they could not be allowed to stand unchallenged. The business community was determined to do battle regardless of the consequences. The Temporary National Economic Committee, a joint executive-legislative body established in June, 1938, to determine the effects of monopoly on the nation's economy, found corporate executives and bank presidents more than willing to defend their practices in public hearings and to convey their resentment at this latest manifestation of what they considered Roosevelt's rash exercise of executive power.[12] But the strategy for dissuading this President from making big business the villain for all the ills of American economic life never had to be formulated. Hitler's success at Munich in 1938, his callous seizure of Czechoslovakia in the spring of 1939, and his invasion of Poland in September of that same year, coupled with the alarming successes accompanying an earlier Japanese invasion of China, abruptly halted all Depression-related efforts at economic reform and finger pointing. With American security at stake, Roosevelt once again had to change his policies and build a new political coalition to ensure the success of a more aggressive foreign policy. Necessity dictated a new economic partnership with big business to give the United States the necessary military supplies and industrial capacity to fulfill its responsibilities in a growing world crisis.

NOTES

1. Edward S. Mason, ed., *The Corporation in Modern Society* (Cambridge: Harvard University Press, 1959), pp. x, 1–9.

2. For a balanced general survey see Glenn Porter, *The Rise of Big Business, 1860–1910* (Arlington Heights, IL: A. H. M. Publishing Co., 1973).

3. The "great merger movement" is thoroughly treated by Namoi R. Lamoreaux, *The Great Merger Movement in American Business, 1895–1904* (New York: Cambridge University Press, 1985).

4. Robert H. Wiebe, *Businessmen and Reform: A Study of the Progressive Movement* (Cambridge: Harvard University Press, 1962) and his *The Search for Order, 1877–1920* (London: Macmillan & Co., 1967).

5. The standard treatment is Robert D. Cuff, *The War Industries Board: Business-Government Relations During World War I* (Baltimore: The Johns Hopkins University Press, 1973).

6. Thomas C. Cochran, *200 Years of American Business* (New York: Basic Books, 1977), pp. 234–237, quote on p. 234.

7. Arthur S. Link and William B. Catton, *American Epoch: A History of the United States Since 1890,* 2nd. ed. rev. (New York: Alfred A. Knopf, Inc., 1963), pp. 261–271, 347–349.

8. Ibid., pp. 265–266, 268–271 and Clair Wilcox and William G. Shephard, *Public Policies Toward Business* (Homewood, IL: Richard D. Irwin, Inc., 1975), pp. 90–91, 204–213.

9. Link and Catton, *American Epoch,* pp. 377–383.

10. Ibid., p. 384.

11. These are the Federal Securities Act of May and the Glass-Steagall Act of June, 1933. The latter is not to be confused with the Emergency Banking Act passed in March, 1933.

12. William E. Leuchtenberg, *Franklin D. Roosevelt and the New Deal, 1932–1940* (New York: Harper & Row, 1940). Leuchtenberg provides the most balanced account of the New Deals.

2 WORLD WAR II: THE GENESIS OF THE PARTNERSHIP

Roosevelt had always been troubled by the entrenched ideological isolationism that narrowly defined America's foreign policy options. In October of 1937, however, concerned by the deteriorating situation in Europe and China, he decided to make a public appeal to the American people to recognize the dangers facing the country and to argue that we, along with other peace-loving nations, should "quarantine the aggressors." His speech set off a fire storm, sending isolationists to the barricades. They were prepared to do battle over any measure that compromised our neutrality. With that kind of response, he quickly realized that naval and military appropriation bills would be difficult to get through Congress, as senators and representatives weighed the political strength of isolationist groups in their own constituencies before supporting the administration's requests for additional funds.[1] In effect, constructing a political coalition to bring America abreast of its global responsibilities was going to be far more difficult than constructing an economic coalition to rebuild our armed forces.

Personally, Roosevelt had never cut his ties with the business community, particularly with those representatives of big business who readily recognized that the nation was facing new challenges that could not be addressed through ideological hostility toward everything that transpired in Washington since the administration shifted its allegiance from the private enterprise sector to the victims of the Depression in 1935. Even after the demise of the NRA (National Recovery Administration), Roosevelt's first secretary of commerce, Daniel C. Roper, consistently maintained close contact with the corporate community through the influential Business Council. The Council was a group of between forty and sixty-five active chief executives from America's largest corporate firms that served as a sort of informal business advisory cabinet for the Roosevelt administration. Apparently the position papers of this group's executive committee, while generally disapproving of many of Roosevelt's policies, were always internal studies, designed to "correct" or "refocus" administration policy rather than publicly embarrass the President. The language used in these position papers was never harsh and even a busy President recognized that the Council was more inclined to work with his administration rather than against it.

The segments of the business community that did not instinctively engage in confrontational politics or view with horror his deliberate association with the victims of the Depression during the "second" New Deal were the ones who now read Roosevelt's policy shifts with unerring accuracy.[2] They recognized a major shift in emphasis when, in his annual message to the opening of the Seventy-sixth Congress in January of 1939, he deliberately focused upon the threat that totalitarianism posed to democracy and international peace, and then noted: "We have now passed the period of internal conflict in the launching of our program of social reform. Our full energies may now be released to invigorate the process of recovery in order to preserve our reform." This was followed by a chilling reference to "the hourglass [being] in the hands of other nations."[3]

The first visible benchmark of this new economic coalition was the Vinson Naval Expansion Act of May, 1938. It authorized the immediate expenditure of over $1 million to construct a navy capable of challenging the combined fleet strength of Japan, Germany, and Italy.[4] Politically and diplomatically it was too little too late, but economically it marked the beginning of a new era in business-government relations. Public procurement goes back to the American Revolution, but contracts that made the Federal government the sole or prime contractor for whole industrial groups were a relatively new phenomenon. During 1938–1939, it was a practice that rapidly spread to every sector of our industrial society; it made the relief and recovery programs of the "second" New Deal irrelevant faster than they could be dismantled.

Public procurement, however, had another dimension that gave a critical role to corporations that were internationally oriented. In the wake of the Munich Pact of September, 1938, which seemed to signal Europe's inevitable march toward war, there developed a heightened concern for the adequacy of certain natural resources and the safety of communication facilities, particularly in the Western Hemisphere. The first legislative manifestation of this concern was the Strategic Materials Act of June, 1939. In a fundamental sense the government was calling upon corporations in the primary products sector to take measures to ensure an adequate supply of these resources for America in the event of a European war.[5]

"Strategic materials," defined as products considered necessary for the prosecution of a war—and only obtainable outside of the United States—were to be stockpiled and acquired preemptively to lessen their availability to the Axis nations. "Critical materials," products that were available in the United States but considered vital to America's rearmament, were to be similarly restricted.[6]

This concern for the stockpiling of natural resources led to the creation of the Metals Reserve Company and the Rubber Reserve Company. Established as subsidiaries of the Reconstruction Finance Corporation (RFC), which, of course, dated back to the Hoover administration, both companies were given the authority to borrow funds from the RFC to purchase the capital stock of any corporation for the purpose of producing, acquiring, or transporting strategic and critical materials for plant construction, or simply working capital, to assist such corporations engaged in national defense. Both "companies" were staffed by individuals drawn from and trained by U.S.-based extractive companies or tire manufacturing firms with significant foreign acquisition facilities. And both "companies" were being asked to assume prime responsibility for ensuring that the United States had an adequate supply of these natural resources for our own military and naval expansion and, after September 1939, to supply those Allied nations fighting the Axis powers. This ultimately led to the establishment of two other subsidiary corporations of the RFC, the Defense Plant Corporation and the Defense Supplies Corporation, further enlarging the partnership arrangement between corporate America and the Federal government.[7]

At the same time the State Department was actively involved in trying to expand U.S. business control over vital communication facilities deemed essential to our hemispheric security. This included encouraging ITT (International Telephone and Telegraph Company) to expand its telecommunication holdings in Latin America and suggesting that Pan American airlines increase its presence in Latin America even to the point of building runways and enlarging their airport facilities. The U.S. government was prepared to supply some of the funds.[8]

Even more dramatic was the State Department's informal partnership role with several American oil companies in order to protect or expand their facilities in Venezuela and, in the case of Mexico, to improve their relations with the Cardenas government, which had recently expropriated most of the foreign oil holdings in that country.[9]

None of these government initiatives had a high visibility, but the extractive and manufacturing sectors of the corporate world knew that the Roosevelt administration and the Congress, whatever their past loyalties, had no illusions about which segment of the American economy had the technical and managerial skills and the financial resources necessary to transform America into what would soon be called the "Arsenal of Democracy."

Industrial mobilization in the sixteen to eighteen months before Pearl Harbor effectively cemented the partnership between government and business. Initially, corporate America stood on the sidelines, cautiously watching the Roosevelt bureaucracy wrestle with the problem of mobilization and the question of whether that mobilization should be administered by individuals drawn from the business community or a mobilization program that adhered to the managerial style of the "second" New Deal, i.e., one in which the government itself directly controlled the process through some sort of mobilization "czar." That issue delayed the development of an appropriate administrative structure for several years as Roosevelt tried to place corporate executives in key posts yet hedge their authority by fragmenting the mobilization machinery with an assortment of agencies, commissions, and boards of ill-defined or conflicting authority.[10]

Roosevelt first addressed the mobilization issue in August, 1939, when he created the War Resources Board and named Edward Stettinus of U.S. Steel as its chairman. Stettinus proved to be so visibly probusiness that the Board promptly became a political liability to the administration. Roosevelt's solution was to quietly ignore its business-oriented recommendations and look elsewhere for advice without undermining his identification with the corporate world as mobilization became a virtual necessity.[11]

It was not until January 16, 1942, more than a month after Pearl Harbor, that Roosevelt finally succeeded in bringing some order into the administration of the industrial mobilization effort. He established the War Production Board and moved Sears Roebuck's Donald Nelson from the Supplies, Priorities, and Allocation Board into this new agency as chairman. Unfortunately, Nelson's credentials as a big business executive did not make him a tough administrator. He allowed the military to control priorities through the powerful Joint Army and Navy Munitions Board. The result was an uneven industrial expansion that seemed to be scandalously profitable to big business and, most troubling of all, triggered a politically embarrassing congressional investigation by a special Senate committee headed by a virtually unknown Democratic senator from Missouri, Harry S. Truman.[12]

Confronted with negative public scrutiny, Roosevelt moved quickly to reestablish the credibility of the government's industrial mobilization program. On October 3, 1942, he abandoned the balkanization policies of the previous three years and moved decisively toward centralizing the mobilization activities of the Federal government. He appointed James F. Byrnes, then sitting on the U.S. Supreme Court, as the director of the Office of Economic Stabilization. Byrnes, who resigned his seat on the Court, proved his worth in a matter of months. It prompted Roosevelt to create still another agency, the Office of War Mobilization, in May of 1943 and to name Byrnes its Director. The Office of War Mobilization was to "coordinate" all existing war agencies. Fred M. Vinson, a member of the U.S. House of Representatives from Kentucky, replaced Byrnes as head of the Office of Economic Mobilization, thereby placing ultimate control of the management of the mobilization bureaucracy in the hands of two political figures drawn from outside the business community.[13]

Yet, it has to be said that in many respects it was a layered solution that allowed Roosevelt to keep and expand the big business linkage, permitting him to retain the dozens of highly experienced dollar-a-year corporate executives that he had already enlisted in the service of the nation.[14]

Public procurement, however, had another dimension that was to profoundly alter the nature of American economic life. Initially the shock of Pearl Harbor and its implications for our Pacific possessions obscured the fact that large segments of corporate America discovered that they now had only one customer, the Federal government; that they had become, in fact, quasipublic. Obviously this new government-business partnership was presumed to be a temporary wartime arrangement.

But there was more to this association than the exigencies of war. A new climate of opinion was beginning to take shape. If government expanded its influence over business, could not business legitimately expand its influence over government? The former arrangement reflected the realities of war, but the latter arrangement was equally inevitable. The Federal government had to be "pressured" on the allocation of scarce materials or "educated" as to the economic necessity of providing funds for wartime capital investments in defense plants or machinery if the military was to receive a continuous flow of supplies. The administration and Congress had to know that private funds were inadequate to finance a massive expansion of the nation's transportation facilities whether it be "Liberty" ships, or oil and gas pipelines, or railroads. What was happening from 1941 to 1943 was more than the forging of an inevitable but short-term wartime alliance; it was the beginning of a more permanent partnership. The government-industrial alliance had so many strands of interdependence (and conflict) that it rendered obsolete many of the partisan political and economic labels of the previous fifty years.[15]

The size of any business was, of course, determined in large measure by the size of the market it served. When that market was created by the Federal government and its decisions were dictated by the supply requirements of a global war, there was almost no limit to the size of the corporate structure it could spawn.

And corporate America responded with production levels that, by 1942, equaled in value the combined production output of Italy, Germany, and Japan. Bigness became an asset in almost every industry. That which America had criticized, sought to break up or regulate, now became the most important asset of our free enterprise system:

Though convenience and capability determined the pattern, it was reinforced by the compatibility of [Secretary of War Henry L.] Stimson and his associates with the premier industrialists who were their wartime partners. In 1940, when the defense program began, approximately 175,000 companies were providing some 70 percent of the manufacturing output of the United States, and one hundred companies produced the remaining 30 percent. By March 1943, even though twice as much was being produced, that ratio had been reversed. The one hundred companies previously holding 30 percent now held 70 percent of war and civilian contracts, and were still gaining in proportion to the others. . . . The great bulk of federal funds expended on new industrial construction had gone to the privileged one hundred companies.[16]

The redeeming feature of bigness in the corporate world was that it could supply all the military hardware needed to turn the tide of battle in Europe in 1942 and in the Pacific in 1943. This was several years earlier than the best industrial mobilization estimates of our military leaders in the early months of the war. Whether anyone liked it or not, World War II was capitalism's most glorious hour. It was the free enterprise system displaying its muscle, its creativeness, and most impressive of all, its energy. Admittedly, World War II generated enormous profits for corporate America, and in time, many segments of the corporate world would be criticized, challenged, and ultimately investigated for these profits, but not for the moment. In 1942, 1943, and 1944, at least, many in the executive branch and most members of Congress felt that corporate America could do no wrong because it demonstrated its ability to serve a nation burdened with global military and economic responsibilities. It has to be said that labor and agriculture did the same with equal if not greater sacrifice, but labor and agriculture had not been the historic villains in the story of America's economic development. For members of the corporate community, World War II was the perfect justification for all they had been arguing for since the 1890s. And what made the record even more pleasing to them was that it was compiled in the service of a new governmental configuration, a partnership with the military that developed out of the war, the beginning of the military-industrial complex that would generate so much political debate in the '50s.[17]

However, this military-industrial complex was only one aspect of the government's efforts. The initial concerns of the Federal government about acquiring an adequate reserve of "strategic" and "critical" natural resources took on a new urgency as our own needs and those of our allies multiplied. The government moved from a posture of encouraging international businesses to increase their control over oil and communication facilities in the Western Hemisphere, to an active partnership with certain companies. In some cases it was a partnership that developed almost to the point of dominance.

When the Japanese overran the rubber plantations in southeast Asia, the Rubber Reserve Company not only rushed to create a synthetic rubber industry in the United States, but also actively sought new sources of natural rubber in Latin America. It and its successor, the Rubber Development Corporation, both of which were set up as RFC subsidiaries, created a virtual American rubber cartel in order to serve our wartime needs.[18]

The inordinate wartime demand for oil provided the most dramatic example of governmental partnership. It started innocently in April, 1941, seven months before our entry into the war, when James A. Moffett, the president of California Arabia Standard Oil Company (later known as ARAMCO), urged President Roosevelt to offer aid to King Ibn Sa'ud of Saudi Arabia to ensure political stability in that country. He pointed out that the King was experiencing war-induced financial hardship as a result of reduced revenues from pilgrims and custom duties. Roosevelt rejected Moffett's suggestion, but did urge the British government to loan money to the King.[19] Almost two years later, W. S. S. Rogers, president of The Texas Company, and H. D. Colliers, president of Standard Oil of California, came to Washington to urge that the United States extend aid to Saudi Arabia with funds from our wartime Lend-Lease program to check growing British economic influence in the area and to "give some assurance that the reserve of oil in Saudi Arabia will remain under [the] control of Americans; and consequently remain available to [the] American economy and to American naval and military forces in the future." On February 18, 1943, Roosevelt issued an executive order making Saudi Arabia eligible for Lend-Lease. In the months that followed, Secretary of War Henry L. Stimson, Secretary of the Navy Frank Knox, and Secretary of the Interior (and Petroleum Administrator for War) Harold Ickes, pressured Roosevelt to make the U.S. government a part owner in California Arabia Standard Oil Company (ARAMCO). Following the creation of the federally funded Petroleum Reserve Corporation, that agency made an effort to purchase an interest in Standard Oil of California, Texaco, California Arabia Standard Oil Company, and Bahrein Petroleum. This was more than the top executives of the oil companies contemplated or felt comfortable with; they had urged Lend-Lease, not government ownership of their corporate stock.[20]

Nothing came of the effort, but the War Production Board did allow steel and other critical materials to be sent to Saudi Arabia so that the California Arabia Standard Oil Company could build a 50,000 barrel-a-day refinery at Ras Tanura. There was also an effort by the U.S. government to acquire ownership of the pipeline from the

Saudi Arabian oil fields to the Mediterranean and even a proposal to secure an interest in Iranian oil fields from the British.[21]

Significantly, the first "major venture in oil production on foreign soil" by the Federal government was in Canada, the so-called Canol Project, initiated in April, 1942. It involved the development of the Norman Wells in the Canadian Northwest Territory to supply fuel for vehicles involved in the construction of the Alaskan Highway and for American planes operating from Alaskan airfields on a polar supply route to Russia. According to the agreement, Imperial Oil of Canada, an affiliate of Standard Oil of New Jersey, would do the drilling and control the wells and the War Department would build the pipelines, construct the refinery, and handle the distribution. The wartime demand for fuel brought the project into operation in the spring of 1944.[22]

In short, "Between 1942 and 1945, whether through the President, the executive departments (state, treasury, war, navy, agriculture), the subsidiaries of the Reconstruction Finance Corporation, or Lend-Lease, the United States participated in international economic relations to an unprecedented extent."[23]

Obviously, the government's active role can be attributed to the unusual circumstances created by a global war. It was presumed that it would end once the Axis powers were defeated. A similar scenario had existed on a smaller scale in World War I, and when that conflict ended the partnership between business and government quickly terminated, returning the economy to a somewhat modified version of the laissez-faire climate of the prewar years. But that scenario was not going to be repeated. The Depression had profoundly altered the attitude of business toward the Federal government and the attitude of the Federal government—particularly the executive branch—toward business. And World War II had not only created, but really solidified and made viable a partnership between big business and the Federal government that was not going to dissolve when the dozens of temporary wartime agencies of industrial mobilization were abolished.[24]

Loosely speaking, the partnership had two components. There was a domestically focused military-industrial complex and, secondly, a somewhat more subtle, globally-oriented linkage between international corporations controlling critical natural resources and several of the Federal government's executive departments, particularly those with responsibilities that gave them a global orientation. It would be the Federal government's perception of its role in the postwar world that would determine the viability of such partnerships in the immediate future.

Yet, in the midst of this hearty endorsement of what corporate America was doing, there was a persistent, if sometimes countervailing concern, about those corporations that had had contractual ties with German or Japanese companies during the '20s and '30s. This was particularly true of the petroleum, mining, chemical, and pharmaceutical industries where the contractual arrangements seemed to restrict or regulate the access of U.S. companies to raw materials, synthetics, and patents now deemed essential to America's military efforts. Three different congressional committees, a Senate committee on patents, a Senate subcommittee on war mobilization, and the Truman Committee, a special Senate committee investigating the national defense program, each raised embarrassing questions about the apparent willingness of some of this country's most prominent international corporations to enter into business arrangements or even formally structured cartels with foreign companies. The disclosures of the Truman Committee prompted the Antitrust Division of the Justice Department to initiate both civil and criminal actions against several American corporations because of their ties with foreign companies, in some cases accusing them of being in violation of the Sherman Antitrust Act.[25]

In the meantime the State and War Departments, the War Production Board, and the RFC, specifically through its metal and rubber subsidiaries, were encouraging corporations to aggressively pursue virtually any corporate arrangement with foreign companies that would secure vital raw materials that were not available from domestic sources. Standard Oil of New Jersey, through its several affiliates, found itself on both sides of the issue—on the one hand it was being investigated for certain international arrangements with I. G. Farben Company dating back to the '20s, while on the other hand it was being encouraged to enter into similar arrangements during the war to ensure a supply of oil and the necessary refining capacity to serve our military needs.[26]

A strange mix of congressional inquiries and threatened civil or criminal litigation for violations of our antitrust laws on one side, and government initiatives that bordered on a partnership arrangement where vital resources were concerned on the other side, created enormous paradoxes. In the future such inconsistencies in government policy would have to be resolved. International commitments, particularly those involving significant financial or legal risks, were not going to be renewed or initiated after the war until the agencies and branches of the Federal government reached some consensus as to the government's role vis-à-vis corporate America in the postwar economy.

NOTES

1. The annual volumes of the Council on Foreign Relations, *The United States in World Affairs* for the '30s effectively convey the flavor of the isolationist sentiment during these years. See also Selig Adler's interpretative study, *Isolationist Impulse: Its Twentieth Century Reaction* (New York: The Free Press, 1957). Adler labeled it "continental no-nothingism," p. 68.

2. Kim McQuaid, *Big Business and Presidential Power: From F.D.R. to Reagan* (New York: William Morrow & Co. Inc., 1982), pp. 30–36, 63–66. See also Robert M. Collins, *The Business Response to Keynes, 1929–1964* (New York: Columbia University Press, 1981), pp. 62, 80–81.

3. Quote from *The Public Papers and Addresses of Franklin D. Roosevelt* (New York: Macmillan Co., 1941), 1939 vol., pp. 1–12, quotes on p. 7. For context see William L. Langer and Everett S. Gleason, *The Challenge to Isolationism, 1937–1940* (New York: Harper Brothers, 1952), pp. 46–48.

4. Arthur S. Link and William B. Catton, *American Epoch: A History of the United States Since 1890,* 2nd. ed. rev. (New York: Alfred A. Knopf, Inc., 1963), p. 477.

5. Mira Wilkins, *The Maturing of Multinational Enterprise: American Business Abroad from 1914–1970* (Cambridge: Harvard University Press, 1974), p. 253.

6. Francis Walton, *The Miracle of World War II: How American Industry Made Victory Possible* (New York: Macmillan Co., 1956), p. 45.

7. U.S. Bureau of the Budget, *The United States at War: Development and Administration of the War Program by the Federal Government* (Washington: G.P.O., 1946), pp. 26–27 and Wilkins, *The Maturing of Multinational Enterprise*, pp. 253–255.

8. Wilkins, *The Maturing of Multinational Enterprise*, pp. 256–257.

9. Ibid., pp. 255–256.

10. McQuaid, *Big Business and Presidential Power*, pp. 67, 69–73 and U.S. Bureau of the Budget, *The United States at War*, pp. 51–52.

11. McQuaid, *Big Business and Presidential Power*, pp. 69–72.

12. Link and Catton, *American Epoch*, pp. 522–523.

13. U.S. Bureau of the Budget, *The United States at War*, pp. 371–397; McQuaid, *Big Business and Presidential Power*, pp. 90–93; and Link and Catton, *American Epoch*, p. 523. Vinson had sponsored the Naval Expansion Act of 1938 that bears his name.

14. U.S. Bureau of the Budget, *The United States at War*, pp. 397–398.

15. Harold G. Vatter, *The U.S. Economy in World War II* (New York: Columbia University Press, 1985), pp. 148–149; U.S. Bureau of the Budget, *The United States at War*, pp. 112–127, 133; Collins, *Business Response to Keynes*, pp. 80–81; and McQuaid, *Big Business and Presidential Power*, pp. 69–72, 77–85, 92–95.

16. John M. Blum, *V Was For Victory: Politics and American Culture During World War II* (New York: Harcourt, Brace, Jovanovich, 1976), pp. 118–123, quote on p. 123.

17. Walter Adams and Horace M. Gray, *Monopoly in America: The Government as Promoter* (New York: Macmillan Co., 1955), pp. 101–116.

18. Wilkins, *The Maturing of Multinational Enterprise*, pp. 269–270.

19. Ibid., pp. 249–250.

20. Ibid., pp. 276–278, quote on p. 277.

21. Ibid., pp. 278–280.

22. Ibid., pp. 273–276.

23. Ibid., p. 281.

24. Collins, *The Business Response to Keynes*, pp. 80–81.

25. Wilkins, *The Maturing of Multinational Enterprise*, pp. 257, 260, 263–267. Wilkins most appropriately observes in an explanatory footnote that the inquiries of the Truman Committee focused on contractual relationships rather than on foreign investments *per se*. This is not to say that the companies being investigated confined their foreign business activities exclusively to contractual relationships.

26. Ibid., pp. 265–266.

3 THE POSTWAR YEARS: 1946–1959

Inevitably, the immediate postwar years found business and government timid partners. The two had worked closely during the war when the threat was real and the goals clear. But the postwar years imposed different agendas on government and business. Defining the agendas of each involved backing away from the wartime partnership before deciding the if, when, and how it should be resumed.

The first issue for testing the waters was a congressionally sponsored measure to make full employment a fixed component of our postwar economy. In January, 1945, a bill aimed at achieving this objective was introduced by Senator James E. Murray, Democrat of Montana. In essence, it addressed the issue of postwar depression, a common concern of both business and labor; however, it did so in a manner that disturbed the business community. The idea of the Federal government assuring "the existence at all times of sufficient employment opportunities" was simply too "New Dealish" for even the most liberal element of the business community. Their response ranged from uncompromising hostility to more temperate efforts aimed at stripping the bill of its Keynesian features. The result was the transformation of a bill guaranteeing full employment into a bill of more modest goals. The Employment Act of 1946 provided for the creation of a Council of Economic Advisors to counsel the President and Congress on the most appropriate means of promoting growth and prosperity.

The serious differences of opinion evident in the thirteen month debate on this measure, however, should not be allowed to obscure the fact that all parties, except perhaps the extreme right in the business community, recognized that, in the last analysis, the Federal government had ultimate responsibility for maintaining economic stability. It was a frame of reference that the progressive element of the corporate community had come to accept as inevitable.

The 1945–1946 debate was domestically focused, but it did initiate the postwar redefinition of the rolls of business and government vis-à-vis economic problems.[1] As Edwin Nourse, the first chairman of the Council of Economic Advisors, observed, the act established machinery for "mobilizing all our organizational resources, public and private, within our system of free enterprise, for a sustained level of national production and a correspondingly high level of national income."[2] If the annual reports of the Council frequently fell short of being a guide to administration policy, they were at least a window into that policy.

Wartime planning with respect to the postwar economy outside of the United States was another matter. It envisioned relief and recovery programs for Europe and our allies in Asia, but nowhere was there a blueprint for making corporate America a partner in the reconstruction of the world's economy. Initial relief, in the form of food, medical care, shelter, and other emergency civilian services was accomplished through Lend-Lease assistance and through the armed forces' civilian supply programs. These programs were supplemented by the United Nations' Relief and Rehabilitation Administration. The United States extended a special loan to Britain in 1946 and then subsequently provided additional relief moneys when the United Nations' Relief and Rehabilitation Administration's funds began to run out in 1947.[3]

The enormity of the relief effort requested by the executive and approved—with some substantive reservations—by Congress was the first chapter in a saga that extended into the '90s. It had a message that the public and private sectors dared not ignore; namely, that we could not sustain such a continuous drain on our resources. Our wartime allies, our former enemies, our current and potential friends, had to be moved off America's global relief rolls and encouraged to marshall their own resources to revitalize their own economies. Relief without recovery, as Roosevelt's New Deals had already demonstrated, was a bottomless pit.

Within the private sector, only the broadly focused Committee for Economic Development (CED), a group of corporate executives, bankers, lawyers, and academicians with a decidedly international point of view, was looking beyond the "relief" aspects of the postwar world and asking a different set of questions about the future. Formed in 1942 by confirmed internationalists Paul Hoffman and William Benton, the CED's instrument of incorporation revealed its ambitious objectives:

To foster, promote, conduct, encourage, and finance scientific research, education, training, and publication in the broad field of economics in order that industry and commerce may be in a position in the postwar period to make their full contribution to high and secure standards of living for people in all walks of life through maximum employment and high productivity in our domestic economy.[4]

The CED's global perspective was established in 1945. In September it published "International Trade and Domestic Employment," subsequently referred to as the Hoover Report. It had been written under the careful supervision of Professor Calvin Hoover of Duke University. To the surprise of many, this corporate-financed study dramatically disassociated the CED from all forms of isolationism and recommended that America play a leading role in programs that would expand international trade and free that trade from some of the constricting and objectionable forms of national control.

The report's liberal and international perspective triggered support within the business community for the previously established International Monetary Fund (IMF) and the International Bank for Reconstruction and Development (World Bank). There was not a landslide endorsement of either agency, yet there was evidence that certain influential segments of the American business community had been converted to internationalism, politically as well as economically. Along with select contacts within the State Department and segments of the international banking and legal community, the CED was considered a part of what ultimately came to be considered the "foreign policy establishment" in America,[5] involved in what Dean Acheson described as a "discovery process":

Only slowly did it dawn upon us that the whole world structure and order that we had inherited from the nineteenth century was gone and that the struggle to replace it would be directed from two bitterly opposed and ideologically irreconcilable power centers.[6]

The first visible policy shift marking the ideological confrontation between Russia and the West came on March 12, 1947, when President Truman asked Congress to provide economic and military aid to Greece and Turkey to assist the governments of these two countries to resist Communist aggression. Truman's request marked the beginning of a shift from a policy that focused on relief and rehabilitation of the victims of war-torn Europe to a policy that explicitly identified Russia as a threat to the free world and initiated the first phase of a policy of containment. Truman was blunt:

I believe that it must be the foreign policy of the United States to support free peoples who are resisting attempted subjugation by armed minorities or by outside pressures. . . . The free peoples of the world look to us for support in maintaining their freedoms. If we falter in our leadership, we endanger the peace of the world—and we shall surely endanger the welfare of our own Nation.[7]

The next moves were even more dramatic. At a Harvard address in June of 1947, Secretary of State George C. Marshall offered to make the United States a major partner in the economic recovery of Europe, if they would assist in the task of their own reconstruction and submit a comprehensive program for lasting recovery. Western Europe responded with enthusiasm, appointed a Committee of European Economic Cooperation, and within a matter of months had a master plan available for the United States. Meanwhile the Congress and the executive branch were aggressively studying both the foreign and domestic aspects of the so-called Marshall Plan.[8] Of the three Presidential committees appointed to study various aspects of the problem, one was a committee of private citizens headed by Secretary of Commerce W. Averell Harriman, which addressed the issue of America's capacity to undertake a large foreign aid program. Joining Harriman on the committee were nine businessmen, five of whom were members of the CED, including its chairman, Paul Hoffman of Studebaker Motors, one of the founders of the CED.[9]

To the surprise of many outside of government, the Marshall Plan soon picked up widespread support from the business community, including the National Association of Manufacturers, the U.S. Chamber of Commerce, and, as might be expected, the small but influential CED.[10] It was common knowledge that much of this support reflected a concern over Communist expansion in Europe, evidenced by the overthrow of a pro-Western coalition government in Czechoslovakia in February, while the measure was still pending before Congress. And there was also a concern over a possible Communist victory at the polls in Italy on April 8 if the measure failed to secure House approval before that date.[11]

After several months of protracted debate in Congress, the European Recovery Plan (ERP), drawn up by the major nations of Western Europe and the United States, came into being on April 3 with the passage of the Economic Cooperation Act of 1948.[12] Although it attracted little public attention at the time, one feature of the ERP gave a new dimension to business-government relations. The Administrator of the Economic Cooperation Administration was authorized to make guarantees of up to $300 million on U.S. private investments. It was, even by 1948 standards, a modest amount, yet there was the perception that business had a role to play and that that role might well expand as Europe became a more attractive investment area.[13]

But it was one thing for the business community to support the European Recovery Program in Congress and still another to take advantage of its provision for investment guarantees. From the point of view of private investors, the climate was far from reassuring. In June, 1948, Soviet and East German troops blocked all land routes to Berlin in retaliation for American, British, and later French moves to facilitate the formation of a West German government. The Berlin Blockade was followed by the establishment of the North Atlantic Treaty Organization (NATO) in August of 1949, making Europe the central battleground in the Cold War. Two months later, the Mutual Defense Assistance Program (MDAP) was implemented. It sent a negative message to the business community. Providing military aid to the European members of NATO as well as to Greece, Turkey, Iran, Korea, and the Philippines suggested the postwar world was not a particularly friendly place for any kind of direct foreign investments.[14]

Investment guarantees acquired an even greater visibility when Congress implemented Truman's Point IV program in June of 1950. First proposed in January, 1949, Truman suggested that the United States assist in a "bold new program for making the benefits of our scientific advances and industrial progress available for the improvement and growth of the underdeveloped areas" of the world.[15] As he noted at a press conference after the program was announced:

I knew from my study of American history that this country was developed by the investment of foreign capital by the British, the Dutch, the Germans, and the French. These countries invested immense sums in the development of our railroads, mines, oil lands, and the livestock industry. . . . After two world wars, in each of which the United States was used as a source of supply for munitions and materials by the European countries, the invested funds in the United States of Britain, Holland, Germany, and France were depleted. . . .

It seemed to me that if we could encourage stabilized governments in underdeveloped countries in Africa, South America, and Asia, we could encourage the use for the development of these areas some of the capital which had accumulated in the United States. If the investment of capital from the United States could be protected and not confiscated, and if we could persuade the capitalists that they were not working in foreign countries to exploit them but to develop them, it would be to the mutual benefit of everybody concerned.[16]

The landmark piece of legislation implementing the Point IV program was the Act for International Development, passed in the spring of 1950.[17]

It was no coincidence that Congress accepted Truman's Point IV program after the National Security Council had quietly promulgated in April, 1950 "NSC 68" within the government. This critical policy paper argued that American policy had to be formulated on the assumption that the Soviet Union was engaged in a systematic effort to seize control of governments in the free world and that it was incumbent upon the United States to assist friendly nations anywhere in the world if threatened by Soviet-backed insurgents.[18] "NSC 68" seemed to make the Cold War a global rather than a European or a Far Eastern confrontation.

On June 25, 1950, literally days after the Point IV program was authorized, the armies of North Korea launched a massive attack on South Korea, giving America what it did not want, a "hot war" in an increasingly demanding "cold war" climate. The war gave a new direction to American foreign economic policy and a new urgency to a broad spectrum of Cold War problems. The scope and tentativeness of it all was revealed in the language of the report of the President's Council of Economic Advisors, transmitted by Truman to Congress in January of 1951:

In some cases [i.e., areas of the world threatened by Communist penetration rather than Soviet aggression], well-designed assistance in expanding production, even of goods unrelated to military strength, can contribute to the essential aspects of common security. . . .

But the common danger and the greatly increased strain on our resources call for reappraising and, if necessary, altering the character and time focus of such programs. . . .

Expansion of productive capacity [in underdeveloped countries] calls for private capital investment, and public investment by the Export-Import Bank and the International Bank for Reconstruction and Development. Grants for technical assistance and, in some critical areas, capital development, will be necessary. Despite present international tensions, measures to facilitate private investment can still be effective in certain areas and are particularly needed to expand raw material production. It is desirable to enact legislation authorizing guarantees to private capital against certain risks peculiar to foreign investment, and to continue efforts to negotiate investment treaties.[19]

Although government risk-sharing programs had been in place for six years, they had failed to stimulate significant foreign investments. Total foreign investments amounted to a little more than $1 billion a year and much of that sum was in oil and other raw material industries.[20] It was a situation that created a serious dilemma for the Truman administration. Renewed debate over the establishment of the Mutual Security Agency in 1951 (replacing the Economic Cooperation Administration) demonstrated how conscious Congress had become of the tax burden imposed on the American people by its foreign aid and now military assistance programs. Funds were being appropriated on a yearly basis, and every request for renewal prompted loud demands for substantial cuts, or assurances that they would not continue indefinitely. Critics of massive foreign aid in Congress argued that if the private sector did not assume a larger role in sustaining Europe's growing economic stability and in supporting the expanding economic aspirations of the Third World, all that had been accomplished to date might well be lost.[21]

As early as 1950, Truman's annual *Economic Report of the President to Congress* made a pointed reference to relaxing America's tax laws to stimulate foreign investment. This report also urged that technical assistance programs, particularly in underdeveloped areas, should be used to promote "concrete development projects" that would make the countries involved more attractive to private foreign investments.[22]

A further concern to the Truman administration was the changing profile of our balance of payments. As Europe's economy slowly recovered, the quantity and value of its goods and services increased while foreign demand for American goods and services declined. Emerging trade patterns suggested our domestic economy would be obliged to adjust to a more competitive climate. The ultimate effect of increased imports and decreased exports on American foreign investments remained clouded in 1951 and 1952, but the Commerce Department and the President's Council of Economic Advisors knew the changing pattern in our balance of payments would bear watching.[23]

Within the government bureaucracy, an interesting sequence of policy decisions with respect to five American oil companies was being made.[24] The way the issue was ultimately resolved taught the corporate world much about the intricacies of government policy making. The story began in 1940–1941, when a grand jury subpoenaed the documents of several American oil companies, allegedly uncovering a world-wide oil cartel involving seven major oil companies, five of which were American. World War II suspended any further investigation of these companies, but with the end of hostilities in Europe and the Middle East in 1944, the investigation was resumed.

In 1951, the Antitrust Division of the Justice Department and the Federal Trade Commission concluded that an oil cartel did, in fact, exist. The Attorney General recommended to the President that the administration pursue the matter further through the grand jury process to determine if the companies in question were in violation of the Sherman Antitrust Act of 1914. Truman asked the State Department for their views on the matter and was told that it was not appropriate for the State Department to interfere in the execution of the antitrust laws but that the implementation of grand jury proceedings certainly would not help the achievement of the foreign policy aims of the United States in the Middle East and had the possibility of seriously impairing their attainment. In spite of this warning from the State Department, Truman gave his approval for a grand jury investigation. The initial proceedings generated enough reaction to cause the State Department to change its position and urge a further review of the matter, arguing that the investigation was making it more difficult to deal with the political unrest in the Middle East—a situation that suddenly acquired greater urgency as a result of the increased strain on domestic oil reserves because of the Korean War. The April, 1951, nationalization of Iranian oil by the government of Muhamed Mossadegh only further complicated the issue.

The State Department's abrupt reversal of its position triggered a cabinet-level debate in the final weeks of the Truman administration and the issue was referred to the National Security Council (NSC) early in January of 1953. In the NSC, the Departments of State and Defense, later joined by the Department of the Interior, and individually by the Chairman of the Joint Chiefs of Staff, General Omar Bradley, argued that Middle East oil was vital to American security and a grand jury probe resulting in criminal indictments against the oil companies would only fuel anti-American feelings throughout the world. The three departments admitted that antitrust action could not simply be dropped without totally compromising America's position as the West's most visible advocate of competition within the free enterprise system. Better, they argued, to proceed through a low-profile civil suit that might get resolved through consent decrees, rather than criminally prosecute international companies engaged in "capturing" a vital raw material for the free world.

The report of the three departments further recommended that the President appoint a commission consisting of the Secretaries of State, Defense, Commerce, and the Interior to give careful attention to the interrelationship among antitrust, security, and foreign policy objectives where petroleum resources were concerned. The commission should provide the Attorney General with guidelines within which he might pursue civil cases. The Attorney General's office responded that the oil cartel was damaging to U.S. interests and that a criminal case was not only necessary from a legal point of view but also would be more decisive. On January 12, 1953, Truman notified the Attorney General that in spite of the recommendations of his department, the Antitrust Division was to proceed through a civil rather than a criminal case. On April 21, 1953, the Eisenhower administration filed a civil suit against Exxon, Mobil, Socal, Texaco, and Gulf. Shell and the Anglo-Iranian Oil, being "foreign" companies, were beyond the reach of American antitrust laws. They were, however, named in the suit as coconspirators.

While this was going on, both the State Department and the British Foreign Office were urging the immediate formation of a multinational consortium of the same seven oil companies to reactivate Iranian oil production after the downfall of the Mossadeq government. The companies, having only barely escaped criminal proceedings at the hands of Truman's Justice Department, insisted on antitrust immunity as a condition for forming the consortium. After NSC review, Eisenhower's Attorney General, Herbert Brownell, was persuaded to write the President on January 21, 1954, endorsing the consortium, a *de facto* grant of antitrust immunity. Brownell's letter undermined the government's current civil suit, at least insofar as it involved production, as opposed to marketing, procedures. The Cold War was beginning to bring antitrust, one of America's cherished obsessions, into question as the policy makers found themselves obliged to create a consortium of multinational oil companies to implement America's foreign policy objectives with respect to "capturing" foreign oil reserves. It was a lesson not lost on the business community.

1953 ushered in the first Republican administration since Herbert Hoover turned over a psychologically paralyzed economy to FDR in 1933. Two Democratic presidents in those twenty years had not only redefined the role of the government in the domestic economy but the role of the United States in the global economy. The economic dimensions of the two New Deals and Truman's Fair Deal suggested many things: regulation, paternalism, presidential initiative, reciprocal trade, higher taxes, a quantum leap in the government's bureaucracy, an essentially prolabor posture, and an ideological, if not substantive, commitment to antitrust. But nowhere was there any hint of openly subsidizing foreign investments. Ties with the business community were substantial, and there was no doubt that both presidents brought many of its successful executives into the government at the highest level of policy making. It was also true that there was a military-industrial complex that had made the United States a world power and revitalized the military establishment of our European and Asian allies. Security considerations, however, had given this association an obsessively domestic focus, for military contracts were only awarded to American-owned and -operated companies.

The fact of the matter was that, aside from the extractive industries, America had few multinationals in 1953 outside of Canada and Latin America, and nothing Truman had said or done had lured corporate America to make substantial investments in Europe or the Third World. When asked, businessmen cited American tax policy on foreign income as the reason for not venturing outside the United States.[25] Yet some form of credits against foreign income taxes had been in place since 1918 and there was little substantive evidence to prove that American tax policy was a deterrent. The ultimate reason seems to have been the absence of economic incentives. The business community firmly believed that substantial growth and profits could be achieved in the United States and nothing the Truman administration had said or done made foreign investments more attractive.

The presumption was that business would be more relaxed about business-government relations with Eisenhower in the White House and a Republican and conservative-Democratic coalition in Congress. But whether the Eisenhower administration intended to promote foreign investments as a means of assisting in the revitalization of the world economy remained to be seen.

The first indication of the thinking of the administration was a telling modification in the Mutual Security Act for 1951. The Mutual Security Act for 1953 recommended the repeal of the free enterprise amendment in the 1951 act. It was this amendment that encouraged private enterprise to enter into the development of the resources of nations that were recipients of funds under the Mutual Security Program. In place of the free enterprise amendment was a provision declaring it to be United States policy to encourage the recipient nations to foster private incentives and competition and to have these nations encourage American private investments in their countries.[26] Truman's risk-sharing mechanism remained in place, but it was not stressed.

And there were more proposals coming. Eisenhower, believing that the aid programs, and particularly the Marshall Plan, had served their purpose and ought to be abandoned, indicated he felt this "patchwork of statutes" should be completely revised.[27] He promised to transmit his recommendations to Congress in 1954.

When the requisite administration spokesmen appeared before the congressional committees to argue for funds for the Mutual Security Program for the current fiscal year, they confronted a Congress critical of continued foreign economic aid to Europe and preoccupied with the amounts allocated for our economic and military assistance programs in the Far East.[28] These congressional hearings publicized several disturbing findings. On June 6, the House Foreign Affairs Committee released a preliminary report prepared by its Subcommittee on Foreign Economic Policy that maintained that the efforts of the Mutual Security Agency as well as other foreign aid agencies to stimulate American investments abroad had not been particularly successful.[29] Then, when the Senate Foreign Relations Committee opened hearings on the Mutual Security bill, they found the chairs at the witness table filled by members of a businessman's task force that had been sent to Europe to evaluate the Mutual Security Program. Its chairman, Clarence Francis, the chairman of the board of General Foods Corporation, recommended abolishing the Mutual Security Agency, turning over its foreign aid functions to the State Department and giving the Defense Department primary responsibility for military assistance. The leader of the evaluating team that went to Italy, Frederick C. Crawford of Thompson Products (later the TRW Corporation), also recommended eliminating economic aid and concentrating on military assistance. The heads of each evaluating team had essentially the same message—end or drastically cut foreign aid and do not over-extend ourselves as a nation with respect to military aid. There was no emphasis given to foreign investments, even as an alternative.[30]

Eisenhower's businessman's task force obviously did not speak for the business community, yet these knowledgeable corporate executives were well aware of the implications of the global rivalry between the United States and Russia. The result was that the Mutual Security Act as it passed both houses of Congress in July, 1953, had a 1955 termination date for the Mutual Security Program, a 1956 termination date for the liquidation of all economic spending, and a 1957 termination date for halting all military spending under the program.[31] Congress was listening to its constituents—and to Eisenhower's businessman's task force.

Eisenhower's first economic report to Congress was sent to Capitol Hill in January, 1954; it reflected a more generalized analysis of foreign economic problems than those prepared by Truman's Council of Economic Advisors. The focus was on domestic policy with only passing references to foreign economic policy. The sense of urgency and the theme of the virtual inevitability of our dominant role in world affairs were dropped in favor of a vague and rather imprecise statement about our general responsibilities. There had been progress toward a "free world economy" and "a broadly balanced pattern of trade and payments and a high and growing level of economic activity," due in large measure to the virtual recovery of Europe. The "State," the Council of Economic Advisors observed, was receding because the trading system of the free world was increasingly being conducted by private enterprise rather than government, an obvious improvement over what had prevailed since the end of World War II. It was something that should be encouraged by the reduction of trade barriers. "At the same time," we should remove "restrictions" on the movement of private capital so that "it [private capital] may play a fuller role in developing new sources of materials, creating new productive facilities, and contributing to an increase in standards of living throughout the free world."[32]

A President with far more international experience than his predecessors chose to make his first annual economic report to Congress little more than a vague statement of America's economic objectives formulated in an essentially domestic perspective. The business community, which had come to view these annual economic reports as important policy statements, found little of substance in the international aspects of Eisenhower's first report.

More useful was the orientation of the administration's foreign trade policy. Reciprocal trade was a New Deal policy that, in principle at least, most Democrats viewed with pride and most Republicans viewed with alarm. By the '50s, some form of reciprocal trade was probably inevitable, but those with a protectionist frame of reference felt that quotas, or some type of "escape clause," should be built into any new legislation suggested by a Republican administration.[33] Eisenhower chose to take a different tack. He asked Congress for another one-year extension of the existing act pending a "thorough and comprehensive" reexamination of "American foreign economic policy."[34]

Although many Republicans were disappointed, they took his request as an indication that 1954 would be the year that the administration would reassess not just reciprocal trade but all foreign economic policy issues—i.e., trade, tariffs, currency convertability, the political and economic stability of our trading partners, foreign economic aid, mutual security, restrictions on trade with Communist bloc countries and their Third World allies, and private foreign investments.

The first step in this reassessment came in August of 1953 with the appointment of the Randall Commission, composed of five senators, five representatives, and seven "public members," presided over by Clarence B. Randall, the chairman of the board of Inland Steel Corporation.

The commission submitted its report in January, 1954. It recommended terminating grants of economic aid, endorsing only "soundly administered" technical assistance programs, and explicitly urging an increase in U.S. private foreign investments as an alternative to U.S. aid. The "government should make clear" its principles for establishing a better climate for such investments. Specifically, the commission urged continued efforts to negotiate treaties ensuring fair treatment of foreign investments, and it also sought two specific changes in U.S. tax law. The changes recommended were a 14 percent reduction of taxes on all income from foreign investments and the removal of certain existing restrictions on foreign tax credits. To the consternation of many protectionist-oriented businessmen, the commission also recommended a continuation of the President's power to negotiate reciprocal trade agreements and, in certain instances, even proposed defining his authority more broadly than had been allowed under the original law of 1934. The commission further suggested that federal aid be provided to certain sectors of our domestic economy that were being adversely affected by our trade policy and urged that special care be taken to protect U.S. workers from unfair competition.[35]

A little more that two months after the Randall Commission released its report, the President sent a foreign aid message to Congress consistent with the commission's recommendations. Neither the Senate nor the House held hearings on the commission's report, citing a heavy schedule as its excuse. Instead, Congress granted the President another one-year extension of his authority to enter into reciprocal trade agreements.[36]

As so often happens, the debate outside of Congress was more interesting than the debate in Congress. The very existence of the Randall Commission generated reaction from hundreds of national organizations and companies. It caused divisions within the U.S. Chamber of Commerce, the National Association of Manufacturers, and the AFL-CIO. The Committee for a National Trade Policy became the voice of internationally-oriented business leaders, bankers, and key partners in some of the prestigious law firms. They were quick to call for a five-year extension of the President's authority to negotiate reciprocal trade agreements, but they were suspiciously silent about foreign investments.[37]

By this time the broad outlines of the administration's policies were becoming evident. There were continued signs of token encouragement of foreign investments, but there were no visible policies that clearly signaled that this administration wanted business to take the lead in furthering "mutual security" in Europe, in Asia, or in the Third World.[38] Foreign investments in Canada, Latin America, or in countries where scarce raw materials could be found were taken for granted, deserving of casual reference where appropriate. Yet they were not a part of this administration's basic policies. At the end of 1954, Eisenhower did issue an executive order establishing the Council on Foreign Economic Policy (CFEP). It was charged with the responsibility of coordinating and developing a "foreign economic policy," a concept that, in theory at least, could include the encouragement of private foreign investments. That the CFEP efforts seemed to have little effect may be explained by the fact that the business community never really indicated it wanted a more aggressive policy. Business looked to this administration for tax relief, for a helpful trade policy, but not for a formal policy on foreign investments. Only the multinational oil companies and other extractive industries expected a partnership arrangement, but they wanted that of any administration, whether Republican or Democratic.

Although the annual economic reports of the President contained references to the encouragement of private foreign investments, they proved to be little more than commitments to a concept rather than to specific plans. And often they seemed to have been included in an effort to make the various aspects of the administration's foreign aid program more palatable to Congress.[39]

The Mutual Security Act of 1955 was the first piece of legislation to clearly reflect the changing focus of foreign aid.[40] Even before the bill was reported out of the Senate Foreign Relations Committee, the President had restructured the program. By executive order he transferred the functions of the Foreign Operations Administration, the administrative arm of the Mutual Security Program, to the State Department and placed the "military aspects" of the program under the Defense Department.[41] The investment guarantee program came under the control of the newly created International Cooperation Administration, a semiautonomous agency within the State Department. As the bill worked its way through Congress, virtually nothing was said about private foreign investments or about the investment guarantee program supposedly designed to encourage these investments.[42] The 1956 foreign aid debate (for the 1957 fiscal year) was little different from the 1955 debate. The amounts requested were greater and the President seemed to be more involved in the management of the legislative process than previously, but otherwise it all seemed to be part of an endless ritual that occurred in each session of Congress.[43]

By 1956 there was a perception that Russia's overall global strategy was again shifting from a military to an essentially economic emphasis, a focus that Eisenhower's critics insisted was not adequately reflected in the administration's request for funds for the 1957 fiscal year. Nor, they insisted, was there any recognition in the current bill of the possible options open to the administration if the recently proclaimed Arab boycott of American companies doing business with Israel was implemented.[44]

Yet, almost a month before the House Foreign Affairs Committee actually opened hearings on the foreign aid bill, the long-dormant Committee for Economic Development (CED) suddenly became more active in what was otherwise predicted to be a monotonous debate. In February, 1956, the CED said that the United States should expand its "public" investment in underdeveloped countries and that "private" investments by U.S. firms should be encouraged by a 27 percent cut in corporate income taxes on income earned abroad, and urged that consideration be given to a "large [sic] reduction." On April 10, 1956, under the sponsorship of the Point Four Information Service, 150 delegates from 75 different national organizations gathered in Washington for a one-day conference on foreign economic aid. The most prominent of the groups represented at this conference was the CED. Its chairman, J. D. Zellerbach of Crown Zellerbach Corporation, reflecting the general attitude of the conference, characterized the administration's foreign aid package as the "beginnings of an answer to the trade-and-aid focus of Russia."[45] While the foreign aid bill as it emerged from Congress was silent on tax benefits for income earned abroad, it did expand the authority of the investment guarantee program and extended its authority to issue guarantees through 1957.[46] With the approach of a presidential election in November, little more could be expected of Congress.

As Eisenhower's first term drew to a close, the administration's verbal commitment to private foreign investments had not generated much in the way of substantive movement of American capital, technology, or management expertise to Europe, much less other areas of the free world outside the Western Hemisphere. And although Europe had clearly achieved a considerable degree of economic stability, there were few economic incentives for significant foreign investments in these markets unless the corporation had had previous experience in the region. The Third World, with adequate risk insurance, ultimately offered possibilities, but, it would be argued, only after America's technical assistance programs had built the economic infrastructure that would support a private investment venture. The roads, ports, electrical power plants, and sanitation facilities had to come first; and they would have to be completed with public, not private, funds. There were other problems as well. An Arab-Israeli war had resulted in the deliberate blockage of the Suez Canal and, during the same week, Soviet troops were effectively smashing an uprising in Hungary. It was not surprising that corporate America had little enthusiasm for foreign investments outside the Western Hemisphere.[47]

In the ten years following World War II, total private investments, including the reinvested earnings of foreign subsidiaries, were $3,729 billion. Of that figure, $853 billion was invested in Europe, $1,433 billion in Canada, $877 billion in Latin America, and $441 billion in other countries. The last figure reflected principally heavy invest-ments in extractive rather than manufacturing or service industries.[48]

The role of the Federal government in generating even this level of investment is difficult to estimate. Risk-sharing programs were the most visible and consistent; trade policy, through reciprocal or bilateral agreements, was easy to identify but difficult to assess; and tax poli-cy was not sufficiently focused on encouraging foreign investments to make an appreciable difference either way. Antitrust was a deterrent, but more in theory than in practice. In fact, even the supportive features of government policy could not offset the greatest single barrier to foreign investment, namely the continued vitality of our domestic economy in the postwar years. All things being equal, it was considered easier, safer, and more profitable to invest in America.

The first two years of Eisenhower's second term seemed to be buried in studies, reports, and investigations of the foreign aid program and our tariff policy. In both areas the domestic conse-quences of existing policy seemed to be the prime motive for much of the honest or selfish soul-searching that characterized the repeated annual debates on these subjects.[49] The public had lost interest, and the concerned members of the business community had turned the issues over to whomever served as their Washington "observer," which could be anyone from a Washington law firm retained to monitor the slow and complex wheels of the bureaucracy to the U.S. Chamber of Commerce, or some comparable organization.[50]

The debate over the Mutual Security Act in 1957 ran from May through August and established that Congress at least intended to shift from grants to loans in the nonmilitary aspects of the program. The focus of the hearings and the debate in both houses of Congress precluded much attention to private foreign investments.[51]

Eisenhower's 1958 request for a five-year extension of his author-ity to negotiate reciprocal trade agreements was, however, another matter. The context of the request was the checkered historical record of earlier requests for negotiating freedom plus a new and potentially dramatic development in future trade relations between the United States and many of its principal trading partners in Europe.[52]

On March 25, 1957, the Treaty of Rome was signed, establishing the European Economic Community (EEC). The signatories—Bel-gium, France, Italy, Luxembourg, the Netherlands, and West Ger-many—intended to initiate a program that would include the gradual elimination of all tariff barriers among them, eventually establishing an economic association of states known as the Common Market.[53] The Eisenhower administration assumed that the EEC would become a single economic entity in its dealings with the rest of the world, establishing its own common external tariffs on imports to protect its internal economic integrity. The six countries that made up this EEC collectively had purchased nearly $3 billion of our exports the previous year, making it a market that could not be lost, particularly in a period of domestic recession (i.e., 1957–1958). The administration expected several years of difficult negotiations to protect America's access to these markets and wanted greater flexibility in the President's negotiating authority.[54]

In its final form, this reciprocal trade bill provided for a four-year extension of the President's authority and allowed him and his successors to negotiate reductions by one of three rather involved formulae or, under certain conditions, to raise tariffs up to 50 percent above those rates in effect on July 1, 1934. In effect, the law permitted the President to continue a policy of gradually "lowering" tariff barriers to further the free flow of goods in international trade.[55]

Eisenhower's January, 1960, *Economic Report of the President to Congress* had a heavily domestic focus, as might be expected. The recession of 1957–1958 had been turned around, and the 1959 economic profile was more promising and was generally interpreted as a credit to the administration. Since this was the last economic report before the presidential election of 1960, it was only natural that it focused on domestic accomplishments rather than on domestic or foreign problems.[56] An appendix to the report took note of a comparatively recent development that bore watching. The United States had a "large deficit in its balance of payments for the greater part of two years." There were a number of causes, not the least of which was the nation's record on private foreign investments since 1945. U.S. private direct investments "moved up rapidly in 1956 and 1957," very different from previous years, but the "improvement" in the figures was due to "major petroleum and other resource development projects, especially in Latin America and Canada." This movement subsided during the 1957–1958 recession, but in the first half of 1958 the outflow of United States capital *"through new issues of foreign securities and other portfolio investments"* rose in response to the markedly higher level of yields prevailing in foreign financial centers. These capital movements subsequently declined, however, as the United States introduced more restrictive monetary policies.[57]

The report noted that there had been resource-development investments as well as manufacturing and service industry investments, many of them in Latin America and Canada. An appendix to the report indicated that there had been a significant expansion of portfolio investments in 1958 to financial centers outside of the United States, followed by a decline in 1959. No interpretation was placed on the ultimate implications of any of these changes and no reference was made to private direct foreign investments as a factor in an emerging balance-of-payments problem.

There was, however, some activity in Congress that suggested a growing interest in the private foreign investment issue. Two different measures for altering U.S. tax policy on income earned from foreign investments were under consideration. The first, the Foreign Investment Incentives Act, introduced by Representative Hale Boggs of Louisiana, permitted corporations to defer payment of their corporate taxes on their "reinvested foreign business income" until distributed as dividends. The bill passed the House, but the opposition of the Treasury Department and the absence of any real support from the White House prompted the Senate Finance Committee to reject and ultimately kill the bill in August of 1960.[58]

A second measure liberalizing the Internal Revenue Code of 1954 respecting the method of computing foreign tax credits ultimately passed both branches of Congress, receiving only the reluctant endorsement of the Treasury Department. Known as the Internal Revenue Code of 1960, it permitted U.S. firms with foreign income to take a "credit"—as opposed to a "deduction"—on their U.S. tax liability for the foreign taxes they paid, either on a per-country basis or, if it produced a larger tax credit, on an overall basis, i.e., totaling all foreign tax liabilities and using the total as a credit against their U.S. tax liabilities. In spite of Treasury Department concerns over revenue loss, the measure was signed by Eisenhower on September 14, 1960, as the increasingly vituperative Kennedy—Nixon campaign was entering its final weeks.[59]

Depending on one's point of view, these measures either represented an effort to correct a significant omission in the tax law or an effort to create a valuable tax benefit for corporations that were multinational. Whatever the intent, the Eisenhower administration was suddenly identified with creating a tax climate that encouraged foreign investments while still pursuing policies aimed at reducing the balance-of-payments deficit. While these efforts were not explicitly contradictory, they did suggest that this administration had never resolved the question of the appropriate place or role of the corporation in U.S. international economic policy. And while the tax savings that the Internal Revenue Code of 1960 conferred on corporations with foreign operations were not challenged by Kennedy, there was no evidence that the new tax law fit into his overall economic policy.

As the Eisenhower administration drew to a close, the sharp decline of American exports coupled with a dramatic increase in the value of imports, largely from Europe, signaled the emergence of a new issue, a more serious balance-of-payments problem than had been originally anticipated. In the past, direct foreign investments had not been substantial enough to figure prominently in the balance-of-payments issue and portfolio investments had only become significant when foreign capital markets began offering attractive returns. Suddenly, the big unknown was the economic consequence of the Treaty of Rome of 1957. It caused the Eisenhower administration to revise its thinking on the kind of authority needed by the executive to promote reciprocal trade agreements. It also caused some segments of corporate America to revise their market strategy to deal with a new and essentially troubling phenomenon, the EEC. What the Federal government had failed to accomplish over a period of fifteen years through investment guarantee programs, limited tax benefits, selective enforcement of antitrust, the generous funding of the World Bank, the International Finance Corporation, the Export-Import Bank, and the Development Loan Fund of the Agency for International Development, the Treaty of Rome was accomplishing in a matter of months. The virtual cartelization of Western Europe, America's principal market, meant corporate America had to rethink its corporate structure. If it wanted to protect its European markets, it had to get inside the European Economic Community. This, in turn, meant manufacturing and marketing its products within the Community's tariff walls rather than depending on the Federal government to protect its European markets through endlessly renegotiated reciprocal trade agreements. The corporation was being forced to become a multinational entity.

An old idea suddenly had a broad appeal to corporate America. Recognizing the benefits of getting inside the Common Market to secure a hold on their traditional European markets, the internationally-oriented corporate giants moved first. Their success, and it was considerable, caused others to follow. It would only be a matter of time before the idea was judged workable anywhere in the world, anywhere there was a stable economy, responsible government, and a market for the products or services the company offered. And if the

Federal government had needed a partner in the Cold War climate of the immediate postwar years, now corporate America needed a partner. Developments in Europe seemed to suggest that the partnership idea had a future that was more beneficial to corporate America than had been the case up to this time.

NOTES

1. For background and context see Arthur S. Link and William B. Catton, *American Epoch: A History of the United States Since 1890*, 2nd ed. rev. (New York: Alfred A. Knopf, Inc., 1963), pp. 670–671. See also Edwin M. Epstein, *The Corporation in American Politics* (Englewood Cliffs, NJ: Prentice Hall, 1969), pp. 39–40; Karl Schriftgiesser, *Business Comes of Age* (New York: Harper, 1960), p. 91.

2. Edwin G. Nourse, *The 1950's Come First* (New York: Henry Holt, 1951), p. 8.

3. Link and Catton, *American Epoch*, pp. 692–693.

4. Quoted in Leonard and Mark Silk, *The American Establishment* (New York: Avon Books, 1981), pp. 245–246.

5. Ibid., pp. 245–248.

6. Dean Acheson, *Present at the Creation: My Years in the State Department* (New York: W. W. Norton, Inc., 1969), p. 726.

7. Harry S. Truman, *Memoirs of....* (New York: Doubleday & Co., Inc., 1956), II, 106.

8. *Congressional Quarterly Almanac, 1948*, p. 172 (henceforth cited as *CQA*).

9. Ibid.; McQuaid, *Big Business and Presidential Power* (New York: William Morrow & Co., Inc., 1982), pp. 154–159.

10. *CQA, 1948*, pp. 189–190.

11. Link and Catton, *American Epoch*, pp. 710–711.

12. *CQA, 1948*, pp. 170–190; for context see Link & Catton, *American Epoch*, pp. 709–712.

13. *CQA, 1948*, p. 171. See also Hadley Arkes, *Bureaucracy, the Marshall Plan and National Interest* (Princeton: Princeton University Press, 1972), pp. 101–104, 221.

It should be noted that in 1949 the European Recovery Plan was given a one year extension with an additional $150 million in investment guarantees to protect private investments by Americans in ERP countries (*CQA, 1949*, p. 335).

14. For general summary see Link and Catton, *American Epoch*, pp. 712–716.

15. *CQA, 1949*, p. 392.

16. Truman, *Memoirs*, II, 231–232.

17. This was a comprehensive foreign economic assistance measure that included Truman's Point IV program (*CQA, 1950*, pp. 204–217). It should not be confused with the Agency for International Development that will be discussed in Chapter 5.

18. William H. Chafe, *The Unfinished Journey: America Since World War II* (New York: Oxford University Press, 1986), p. 249.

19. "The Annual Economic Review, January, 1951: A Report to the President

by the Council of Economic Advisors," in *Economic Report of the President Transmitted to the Congress, 1951* (Washington: G.P.O., 1951), p. 121.

20. Mira Wilkins, *The Maturing of Multinational Enterprise: American Business Abroad from 1914 to 1970* (Cambridge: Harvard University Press, 1974), pp. 328–331.

21. *CQA, 1951*, pp. 204–211.

22. *Economic Report of the President. . . , 1950* (Washington: G.P.O., 1950), pp. 14–15.

23. See: W. M. Scammell, *The International Economy Since 1945*, 2nd ed. (New York: St. Martin's Press, 1983), p. 20; and frequent references to the subject in the 1951 and 1952 economic reports of the President to Congress (*The Economic Report of the President . . . , 1951* (Washington: G.P.O., 1951) and ibid., *1952* (Washington: G.P.O., 1952).

24. The relationship between the Federal government and five of the major "integrated" American oil companies in the Middle East in the postwar years has been explored from several different perspectives by David S. Painter, *Oil and the American Century: The Political Economy of U.S. Foreign Oil Policy, 1941–1954* (Baltimore: The Johns Hopkins University Press, 1986), pp. 96, 100, 116, 127, 172, 192–198; Michael B. Stoff, *Oil, War, and American Security: The Search for a National Policy on Foreign Oil, 1941–1947* (New Haven: Yale University Press, 1980), pp. 195–196; Walter S. Measday, "The Petroleum Industry," in *The Structure of American Industry*, ed. by Walter Adams (New York: Macmillan Co., 1982), pp. 42–67; Wilkins, *The Maturing of Multinational Enterprise*, pp. 319–323; and Anthony Sampson, *The Seven Sisters: The Great Oil Companies and the World They Shaped* (New York: Bantam Books, 1981), pp. 144–156.

25. J. Frank Gaston, *Obstacles to Direct Foreign Investment: Report Prepared for the President's Committee for Financing Foreign Trade* (New York: National Industrial Conference Board, 1951), pp. 18–19, 22, 359–364.

26. *CQA, 1953*, p. 218.

27. Ibid.; Stephen E. Ambrose, *Eisenhower: The President* (New York: Simon & Schuster, 1984), p. 379.

Eisenhower's first State of the Union message on February 2, 1953 carried a brief reference to private American investments abroad that suggested foreign governments, rather than the United States, should provide the investment climate to encourage investments "doing whatever Government properly can to encourage the flow of private American investment abroad. This involves, as a serious and explicit purpose of our foreign policy, the encouragement of a hospitable climate for such investment in foreign nations." (*The Eisenhower Administration, 1953–1961: A Documentary History*, ed. by Robert L. Branyan and Lawrence H. Larsen (New York: Random House, 1971), I, 93.

28. *CQA, 1953*, pp. 219–224.

29. Noted in ibid., p. 220.

30. Ibid., p. 222.

31. Ibid., p. 223.

32. *Economic Report of the President. . . , 1954* (Washington: G.P.O, 1954), pp. 1–225, quotes and precise references on pp. 108, 110.

33. *CQA, 1953*, p. 211.

34. Ibid., p. 210.
35. *CQA, 1954*, pp. 266–268.
36. Ibid., pp. 269–271.
37. Ibid., pp. 271–272.
38. Burton I. Kaufman, *Trade and Aid: Eisenhower's Foreign Economic Policy, 1953–1961* (Baltimore: The Johns Hopkins University Press, 1982), p. 32.
39. *Economic Report of the President . . . , 1955* (Washington: G.P.O., 1955); ibid., *1956* (Washington: G.P.O., 1956); ibid., *1957* (Washington: G.P.O., 1957).
40. *CQA, 1955*, pp. 301–309.
41. Ibid., p. 304.
Since its inception, foreign aid had been handled by several different agencies: October, 1951–August, 1953, by the Mutual Security Administration; August, 1953–June, 1955, by the Foreign Operations Administration; and June, 1955–November, 1961, by the International Cooperation Administration. See Marina von Neumann Whitman, *Government Risk-Sharing in Foreign Investment* (Princeton: Princeton University Press, 1965), pp. 79–80; *CQA, 1955*, p. 304; and *CQA, 1956*, p. 433.
42. *CQA, 1956*, pp. 301–309.
43. Ibid., pp. 427–431.
Burton Kaufman's cautious review of Eisenhower's foreign economic policy observed:

From the summer of 1954 to the summer of 1955 the Eisenhower administration began to consider alternatives to world economic development other than its stated policy of "trade not aid." In this sense, the year was a transition period for the administration. Trade-not-aid remained its preferred approach to world economic problems, but the White House recognized that in the light of the threat posed by Communist expansion, the program by itself was insufficient to deal with the pressing problems of Third World economic developments (*Trade and Aid*, p. 57).

44. Ibid.; *CQA, 1956*, pp. 418–427.
45. *CQA, 1956*, p. 427.
46. Ibid., pp. 421, 427.
47. Wilkins, *The Maturing of Multinational Enterprise*, pp. 374–397 and Raymond A. Bauer, *et al., American Business and Public Policy: The Politics of Foreign Trade* (New York: Atherton Press, 1967), pp. 112–113.
48. Figures compiled by Whitman, *Government Risk-Sharing in Foreign Investment*, Table 27, p. 331.
49. Kaufman, *Trade and Aid*, pp. 152, 154–159.
50. A careful reading of a newspaper that closely followed the Washington scene would suggest the Eisenhower administration was on the defensive in both areas, although there would be little agreement as to why. The various studies on the foreign aid question—twenty-two authorized by the Senate alone (*CQA, 1957*, p. 604)—suggested that the seemingly endless nature of foreign aid required that it be continuously refocused and repackaged. The reciprocal trade debate was less a matter of repackaging and more a question of trying to build a bipartisan coalition for a five-year extension of the President's authority to negotiate trade agreements.
51. *CQA, 1957*, pp. 601–610.

Testimony before a special committee of the Senate found few witnesses even referring to private investment. Eric Johnson, chairman of the President's International Development Advisory Board, candidly admitted it would take a long time to stabilize the economies of the underdeveloped nations to the point where private investments could take over (ibid., p. 603). Benjamin Fairless of U.S. Steel revived what had become the standard plea of the business community, that to stimulate private investments abroad the government had to reduce the level of taxation on foreign business income (ibid.). But beyond observations such as these, there was little attention given to private foreign investments. The focus was elsewhere.

52. *CQA, 1958*, pp. 165–175.

53. Link and Catton, *American Epoch*, pp. 825–826 for historical context.

54. *CQA, 1958*, p. 591.

55. Ibid., p. 174.

56. *Economic Report of the President...*, *1960* (Washington: G.P.O., 1960), pp. 1–71.

57. Ibid., Appendix B, pp. 81–124; quotes, as they appear in text, on pp. 116 and 113, respectively (emphasis added).

58. The Boggs bill was intended to serve as an incentive to American corporations to invest more heavily in underdeveloped countries. Introduced on January 7, 1959, it acquired additional prominence with the release of the Boeschenstein Report in March of 1959 and the Straus Report in April of the same year. Both reports were supportive of tax incentives for foreign investment. Undoubtedly they helped secure House passage of the Boggs bill in May (*CQA, 1960*, pp. 336–338).

59. Ibid., pp. 339–340.

4 THE CHANGING GLOBAL ECONOMY IN THE TURBULENT '60s

As the Eisenhower administration drifted into its final year, the "spirit of Camp David" invited a cautious optimism about a foreseeable end to the Cold War with expanded economic options opening up for both the East and West. But the downing of an American U2 reconnaissance plane over Russia quickly dispelled that dream. Eisenhower left office with Cold War tensions more visible than they had been in several years. Although Kennedy's style and rhetoric, and his deliberate reliance on a younger group of advisors, may have captured the attention of the American people, thoughtful observers knew that Camelot-style decision making did not solve problems. The change in administrations had no noticeable effect on the global economic picture, leaving the business community largely unenthusiastic about Joseph P. Kennedy's son.[1]

A far more alarming change, particularly for American firms with heavy investments in Latin America, was Fidel Castro's sweeping expropriation of U.S. businesses in 1959 and 1960. When this action was placed in the context of general anti-Americanism in Latin America and corporate awareness that the extractive industries in several South American countries were under pressure from the governments of those countries to share more of their profits, if not their expertise, the glamour and much of the economic justification went out of continued heavy investments in that area.[2] The government-supported Bay of Pigs invasion suggested that the United States would be, at best, an inept partner if American firms turned to Washington for assistance. Symbolically at least, the record did not bode well for the future.

The first hard evidence of Kennedy's attitude toward the multinational corporation came in his balance of payments message to Congress on February 6, 1961, just weeks after his highly quotable inaugural address. Focusing on the ever-increasing deficit in our balance of payments profile, he linked the problem to a whole series of policy considerations. Despite a continued surplus of exports over imports, large outlays abroad for "private investment," "defense purposes," and "economic aid" were producing a deficit. Tangentially linked to his explicit and persuasive-type policies for dealing with this deficit in the balance of payments profile were Kennedy's views on American foreign investment:

> I shall recommend that Congress enact legislation to prevent the abuse of foreign "tax havens" by American capital abroad as a means of tax avoidance. In addition I have asked the Secretary of Treasury to report by April 1 on whether present tax laws may be stimulating in undue amounts the flow of American capital to the industrial countries abroad through special preferential treatment and to report further on what remedial action may be required. But we shall not penalize legitimate private investment abroad, which will strengthen our trade and currency in future years.[3]

As a less significant aspect of his balance of payments policy, it reflected no dramatic shift in American policy toward the multinational corporation. Rather, it flowed naturally out of the policies of the late '50s. If there was a noticeable break, it was with the postwar policies of Truman in deliberately encouraging American investments in Europe to revive the economies of our allies and principal trading partners.[4]

Global economic relations, particularly among the developed nations of the West, were changing much more rapidly than postwar military and political patterns. In fact, the changing economic patterns were forcing a reassessment of the political and military policies that the West had pursued over the past decade.

Far more indicative of the administration's thinking on future global economic relationships was Kennedy's "earnest" request for early Senate confirmation of the Charter that would make the United States a member of the Organization for Economic Cooperation and Development (OECD). Negotiated during the Eisenhower administration, the Charter would bring the United States into closer economic ties with the major developed nations of Europe and provide the country with greater access to Europe's two principal trading blocs, the Common Market and the newly formed European Free Trade Association. Those who supported U.S. participation in the OECD (and it passed the Senate by a vote of 72 to 18) recognized that there had been a significant shift in the nature of our economic relations with Europe. While the balance of payments problem was the most visible manifestation of this shift, the need for a thorough review of tariff rates between the major industrialized countries within the Atlantic Community and the importance of bringing a revitalized Europe into the task of providing economic assistance to the underdeveloped areas of the globe served to justify the OECD.

Corporate America's support for the OECD was channeled through the Chamber of Commerce and the U.S. Council of the International Chamber of Commerce, although the administration's principal spokesmen, Secretary of the Treasury Douglas Dillon and Under Secretary of State George Ball, were instinctively identified with the eastern establishment wing of the business community.[5]

Ratification of the OECD Charter by all twenty signatories by September, 1961, constituted an historic decision by the major industrial nations of the West to act in concert on a broad range of economic issues for their own betterment and for the betterment of less-developed areas of the world. It offered no specific inducements to corporations with international markets, although corporate multinationalization was made much more attractive. While CEOs recognized that a Charter and a Paris-based secretariat did not necessarily justify dramatic changes in the global orientation of any corporation, they were acutely aware of the fact that in recent years (since the signing of the Treaty of Rome in 1957) economic barriers between nations had been giving way to widespread economic consultation and cooperation.

By the early '60s corporate America began to respond to this changing economic climate. Even the so-called Third World was beginning to seem more attractive given the stated commitment of the more prosperous nations of Western Europe to assist in financing the infrastructure necessary to support economic development. The nature of the U.S. role in a growing network of international and regional economic organizations set the stage for an inevitably closer relationship between business and government than had developed in the late '40s or early '50s. Initially, at least, the Kennedy administration neither supported nor repudiated this climate.

For the business community, the international economic priorities of the Kennedy presidency were to be found in the overhaul of the foreign aid program, a revision in the tax law, and a precedent-shattering new trade program. Embodied in each of these efforts was at least an "attitude" toward the multinational corporation that the business community tried to evaluate.

The President's efforts to restructure the foreign aid program pivoted on a new law that, he hoped, would relieve his and presumably subsequent administrations of the burden of seeking annual appropriations from Congress. He asked Congress for the authority to extend economic aid on a multiyear basis in order that the recipient nations might initiate long-term development projects. This request also reflected his awareness of the growing hostility in Congress to economic aid because of the perpetual drain on the nation's tax revenues, a drain congressmen found difficult to justify to their constituents. Kennedy's message of March 22, 1961 tried to invoke the image of the United States being at a "special moment in history" when the "whole southern half of the world" was caught up in the "adventure" of "asserting their independence and modernizing their old ways of life." If the United States was going to assist the nations that were willing to help themselves, it would have to focus its aid not on "annual grants" or "loans" but on long-term "development plans." This required the "divorcement" of military from economic assistance programs and, equally important, provisions for private investment guarantees, which would cover not only losses from nonconvertibility,[6] expropriation, war, and revolution (the language of the existing laws), but also insurrection and civil strife. In addition, Kennedy asked for the authority to issue guarantees of up to $100 million against the loss of a "loan" investment due to nonpayment "for any reason."[7]

He further requested Congress to appropriate $5 million to pay up to one-half the cost of surveys for "investment opportunities by private enterprise."[8] The specific and/or technical nature of this request suggested it reflected the thinking of his economic advisors rather than pressure from the corporate community anxious to see a more specific definition of investment guarantees in place before they committed themselves to greater Third World investments.

The administration's draft bill was introduced into the Senate and House in the last week of May with the Senate Foreign Relations Committee and the House Foreign Affairs Committee holding separate hearings during June and early July. In their testimony before these committees, the President's representatives focused on the long-term financing aspects of the bill, assuming that Congress would be most reluctant to surrender its authority to pass yearly appropriation bills.[9] Only Frank Coffin, director of the Development Loan Fund, specifically addressed the provisions of the investment guarantee program when he said that the government should have the power to help shape the environment in which U.S. private enterprise would assist underdeveloped nations, many of which were "high-risk" areas.[10]

Nonadministration witnesses offered conflicting testimony. The U.S. Council of the International Chamber of Commerce urged the liberalization of the investment guarantee program to encourage more private investment abroad. A spokesman for the Citizens Foreign Aid Committee opposed the administration's measure, insisting that foreign aid actually undermined private investment abroad. It would be more appropriate, this group argued, to grant tax incentives to promote private investment abroad.[11]

The measure came out of the Senate Foreign Relations Committee fairly intact, granting the President most of the things he had asked for. The dollar amounts were changed, but that was to be expected. The Senate generally followed the recommendation of its own Foreign Relations Committee with some further adjustments in the amounts authorized. In neither the Committee nor on the Senate floor did the provisions of the investment guarantee program attract much attention.[12]

In the House, the President's bill acquired an added dimension. The hearings before the House Foreign Affairs Committee produced no new advocates or critics from either within or outside the administration, and a clean bill was reported out of the committee on August 4. There was, however, a potentially significant "declaration" added to the bill by the House Foreign Affairs Committee that had as its object the protection of American firms—multinational or otherwise—trading with Israel. The "declaration" stated that Arab nations that had boycotted U.S. firms either owned by Jews or doing business

with Israel could be denied U.S. aid.[13] Barring or restricting aid to
Communist countries and their allies had been an integral part of
America's foreign aid program almost from the beginning, but never
had a specific group of nations, ethnically identified, been singled out
for possible retribution because of their policies toward another
country or people. Barring foreign aid to countries judged unfriendly
to the United States was one thing, but threatening to withhold aid
from moderately friendly Arab countries with vast oil reserves was
another matter.

The final bill "authorized" $7.2 billion over five years for develop-
ment loans, but insisted that the actual funds would only be provided
through annual congressional "appropriation" bills, precisely what
Kennedy was trying to avoid. Significantly, the declaration aimed at
penalizing Arab nations that boycotted American firms doing business with Israel was dropped. In its place, Congress inserted a
comparatively bland declaration supporting the principles of freedom of navigation and travel without regard to race or religion.[14]

In terms of the investment guarantee program, the Senate-House
conference committee accepted the House version of the levels of
investments and degree of risks that would be covered under the
program.[15] On September 4, the President signed into law the Foreign
Assistance Act of 1961, accepting the inevitable, a five year "authorization" of $7.2 billion, yet still dependent on annual congressional
"appropriation" bills.

The thrust of the President's special message on March 22, and the
refusal of Congress to accept the bill as written, particularly in terms
of insisting on annual "appropriations," kept attention away from
those aspects of the bill that directly affected the multinational corporation. And the fact that the investment guarantee program had
acquired specificity did not necessarily make it more attractive to the
business community.[16] The most interesting aspect of the congressional process was the legislative branch's reaction to the continued
Arab boycott of American firms.[17] It suddenly became evident that
Congress could easily use its tightly guarded authority to pass annual
"appropriation" bills to revive its strong declaration denying aid to
Arab nations that boycotted American firms doing business with
Israel. In effect, Congress had the option of annually redefining
American foreign policy in a vital area of the globe. And there was
nothing corporate America could do about it, even if, as in the case
of the multinational oil companies operating in the Middle East,
such a policy declaration might well endanger their source of supply.

It had become the established practice for the corporate community to keep their lines of communication with the departments of Commerce, Treasury, State, and, of course, the Antitrust Division of the Justice Department open; now it seemed the Senate Foreign Relations and House Foreign Affairs committees had to be kept under closer surveillance, not just to monitor a pro-Israeli or a pro-Arab policy, but to counteract any policy that did not take cognizance of the global political realities within which all international businesses—but particularly the multinational corporations—were forced to operate.

The comparatively low profile of the corporate community on the foreign aid measure as it moved through Congress can be explained in part by the fact that it had no real stake in the issue of annual versus multiyear "appropriations" and no passionate commitment to investment guarantees. But there was another reason. In April of 1961, Kennedy had sent a tax message to Congress suggesting various changes in the existing tax law. Because many of them had been proposed during the Eisenhower administration, from Kennedy's perspective, they lacked the stigma of Democratic sponsorship. The executive branch failed to translate Kennedy's message into a formal tax bill because the administration had an ambitious legislative agenda for 1961. What did materialize, however, was an initial effort by the Democratic-controlled House Ways and Means Committee, under the chairmanship of Wilbur Mills of Arkansas, to draft a bill encompassing proposals that were presumably consistent with the administration's thinking.[18]

In the initial hearings before the Committee in May and June, the business community gave Mills and his colleagues a forceful view of their thinking. Kennedy had poked a hornet's nest and the House Ways and Means Committee suddenly found itself trying to resolve the issue in a manner that still spelt tax reform. As the battle lines formed, everyone waited for an updated version of the President's thinking on tax reform. But the waiting was in vain as the President arbitrarily juggled his legislative priorities.

These priorities were spelled out in January, 1962, in his first annual *Economic Report to Congress*. It was not only what was said, but the context in which it was said, that was important. Kennedy's letter of transmittal focused not on tax reform as many had expected, but on the domestic economy and the extent to which his policies during the previous twelve months had reversed what he considered to be the negative economic climate that confronted him when he took office.

He suggested that the major economic problem facing the nation was really the balance of payments issue, with its consequent drain on the nation's gold reserves:

We must attain a balance in our international transactions which permits us to meet our heavy obligations abroad for the *security* and *development* of the free world without continued depletion of our gold reserves. . . . Simultaneously, we must continue to reduce barriers to international trade and to increase the flow of resources from *developed* to *developing* countries.

And then he spelled out his thinking on foreign investments:

To place controls over the flow of private American capital abroad would be *contrary to our tradition and economic interests*. But neither is there justification for special tax incentives which stimulate the flow of U.S. investment to countries now strong and economically developed, and I again urge the elimination of these special incentives.

And certain forms of foreign investment could be discouraged in another way as well:

The new foreign trade program which I am proposing to Congress will help to reduce another artificial incentive to U.S. firms to invest abroad. The European Common Market has attracted American capital, partly because American businessmen fear they will be unable to compete in the growing European market unless they build plants behind the common tariff wall. We must negotiate down the barriers in trade between the two great continental markets, so that the exports of our industry and agriculture can have full opportunity to compete in Europe.[19]

His approach involved endorsement of foreign investment in principle, correction of the tariff problems that were stimulating it in Europe, and elimination of the tax incentives that encouraged it in all "developed" countries. In effect, the repeated balance of payments deficits were the problem; perhaps adjusting foreign investment practices was part of the solution. The scope of Kennedy's proposed program precluded meaningful ideological opposition or support— at least for the present.

Five days later the President sent Congress his new trade program. His references to the absolute necessity of correcting the balance of payments deficit and the unquestionable need to gain access to the markets of the European Economic Community (EEC) were explicit.[20] By implication at least, everything else was negotiable. In the meantime the House Ways and Means Committee, in executive session, was earnestly revising its 1961 draft of the tax bill,[21] but Kennedy's trade bill captured the headlines. It was a major administration effort that Kennedy insisted be accorded the highest priority in Congress. The hearings before the House Ways and Means Committee and the Senate Finance Committee seemed endless and, as in 1958 when a more modest reciprocal trade extension measure was requested by Eisenhower, many national lobbying organizations were themselves divided on the administration's measure.[22]

In all of this, multinational enterprises did not function as a genre but as individual members of one or more market groups responding to the President's initiatives in terms of how these initiatives might affect them.[23] For many it was not only a question of what powers the President would get, but how effective he would be in using them when the hard negotiations began. And that, in the last analysis, depended on the perceived place of the United States in the overall international economic equation.

The bill that passed, a distinctive move toward greater executive authority in tariff negotiations, was looked upon as a major victory for the administration.[24] It suggested that the President considered trade liberalization the cornerstone of his foreign economic policy, the ultimate success of which would reduce economic aid and would, in conjunction with other policy initiatives, rectify the balance of payments problem.

Congress' efforts to limit or redirect foreign investments through modification of existing tax laws achieved only limited success. The bill that had emerged from the House Ways and Means Committee had numerous provisions with respect to taxing the unrepatriated foreign earnings of American corporations—multinational and otherwise—but the extent to which this orientation reflected the specific intent of the President was difficult to determine. It was impossible to know whether the President was determined to neutralize the tax benefits of foreign investments or whether he really wanted to advance a tax policy that would stimulate the domestic economy. And, although he was consulted, he was not the author of House bill HR 10650, the official designation of the bill as drafted by the House Ways and Means Committee. For the record, he was publicly committed to the investment tax credit provisions of the bill, which had a domestic orientation, and he had issued an executive order liberalizing the existing IRS's schedule of depreciation allowances while HR 10650 was moving through Congress.

Both initiatives were clearly designed to spur the domestic economy rather than impact foreign investments. The tax deferral provisions of existing law were left untouched and the allowance of a U.S. tax "credit" (as opposed to a "deduction") on moneys paid in foreign taxes was kept as well. The only significant adjustment in existing tax law was a provision subjecting to immediate taxation the income of subsidiary corporations (branches) that had been deliberately set up as dummy entities in countries with very low or no taxes on corporate earnings. Characterized as "tax haven corporations," they were, in effect, depositories for the foreign earnings of multinational corporations with subsidiaries in foreign countries that had substantial corporate taxes. It was the only part of the bill that was clearly directed against multinational corporations.[25]

As Kennedy signed the bill into law on October 16, 1962, some eighteen months after he made his original proposals, he described the bill as a "good start" in modernizing the nation's tax structure, providing a "favorable context for the over-all tax reform program I intend to propose to the next Congress."[26] In the final analysis, as Kennedy apparently realized, the measure represented a legislative effort that could not possibly achieve its objectives. The administration had gotten itself closely identified with a bill that was supposed to spur the domestic economy, discourage further foreign investments in developed countries because of our balance of payments problems, yet not discourage investments in underdeveloped or Third World countries where it was clearly needed in spite of the fact that it would add to these balance of payments problems. Such ambitious and somewhat contradictory goals could not possibly be achieved simply by revising the existing tax codes even if this bill's provisions had not been modified as it went through Congress. Yet it was an historic piece of legislation. It was the first law ever passed by Congress and signed by a President that explicitly restricted the incentives of the multinational corporation, i.e., their right (however selfish) to create subsidiary corporations as tax havens wherever they chose.

While the administration focused on trade liberalization and correcting the balance of payments deficit, Congress was changing the climate for foreign investment by addressing the issue of expropriation. It represented the revival of a policy that had been introduced in the amended Mutual Security Act of 1954. The immediate occasion for renewed interest in this matter was the expropriation of ITT property by the governor of the Brazilian province of Rio Grande do Sul. It was a move that brought ITT's aggressive president Harold Geneen to Washington to urge the State Department to send a clear message to all governments contemplating expropriation that such actions would invite a strong response from the administration.

The 1954 and 1959 Mutual Security Authorization acts both carried provisions that suspended foreign aid to the expropriating nation but permitted the President to waive that suspension if American national interest so required. The current proposal, introduced by Senator Bourke Hickenlooper of Iowa and known as the Hickenlooper Amendment (to the 1962 foreign aid authorization bill), denied the President the discretionary authority to continue foreign aid and further stated that discriminatory taxes or restrictive operating conditions that "had the effect" of expropriation would also lead to the suspension of foreign aid. Kennedy opposed the measure, but to no avail.

This bill also raised the ceiling on investments that could be covered under the investment guarantee program and on the total sum of all investments that could be guaranteed by the government. Since it was all part of a bill "authorizing" funds for foreign aid, the President had no choice but to sign the measure in spite of his reservations about many important features of the legislation, including, of course, the Hickenlooper Amendment.[27]

While this bill was going through Congress, the focus of debate was on restricting aid to Communist countries and the usual efforts to reduce and refocus the funds requested. The arguments for or against an expropriation policy did not seem to invite a specific reaction from the business community or the usual lobbying groups on either side of an obviously probusiness proposal. Nor could anyone characterize the Hickenlooper Amendment as blanket protection of the multinational corporation's facilities in countries noted for their political instability. At best, it invited speculation as to how wise it was to have American foreign policy fashioned in response to corporate losses due to expropriation.

With the passage of this foreign aid "authorization" bill in August, 1962, the government, either through the executive or legislative branch, had fashioned a kind of disjointed support mechanism for multinational corporations that was more visible—at least to the internationally-oriented corporate community—than anything that had emerged during the Truman or Eisenhower administrations. The balance of payments problem had also caused the government to fashion an equally disjointed restrictive mechanism that had, at best, a pragmatic justification. Neither business nor government seemed disturbed by the fragmentation or the contradictions that flowed from this no-policy policy.

In 1963 there were numerous reasons for Kennedy to focus on domestic issues and only a continuing balance of payments problem to invite a reassessment of America's private foreign investment policy. Being at heart a politician, Kennedy had to look ahead to the presidential election in 1964 and make an obvious assessment—the domestic problems and the unrest within the Black community would hurt him and his party at the polls while the balance of payments issue was of little interest to the electorate.[28] His annual *Economic Report to Congress* on January 21, 1963 was comprehensive in scope but specific in its priorities. He had a domestic program for Congress to consider, and he intended to make further recommendations to correct the ever-increasing deficit in the balance of payments profile:

> The outflow of private investment funds is influenced by many economic factors, especially the profitability of investment abroad. But it is also influenced by economic activity in the United States. When U.S. capacity is fully utilized, and when capital for domestic investment is in large demand, high profitability will keep capital at home provided that bank credit expansion is not excessive. When capacity is under utilized, unemployment widespread, and the domestic investment outlook discouraging, capital will seek higher profits and interest yields abroad.[29]

In short, if there was a promising investment climate at home, there would be few incentives for Americans to invest abroad.

To assist in making private foreign investments even less attractive, Kennedy tried a new tack. In his second message to Congress on the balance of payments problem in July, 1963, he urged the immediate passage of a temporary interest-equalization tax[30] designed to reduce the flow of American dollars to foreign sources by making the cost of borrowing in America equal to or greater than the cost of borrowing elsewhere. The tax was to be imposed on all U.S. lending agencies on the assumption that it would then be passed along to the foreign borrower in the form of higher interest rates. This was the first time anyone had suggested using the taxing authority of the Federal government to reduce the "capital accounts" deficit[31] (as opposed to the "trade" deficit) in the balance of payments equation. For some, Kennedy's proposal for an interest-equalization tax was a sign of desperation, a recognition that the most obvious methods of correcting the imbalance—reducing overseas defense forces, curtailing economic aid to the Third World, or devaluing the dollar—created more problems than the balance of payments deficit itself.

The House Ways and Means Committee refused to move quickly on the President's proposal and then its urgency was compromised by the findings of a Brookings Institute study. Requested initially by the President's Council of Economic Advisors, the study suggested that there had been too much emphasis on the balance of payments problem and not enough emphasis on the adequacy of the methods used to finance world trade. And in any case, the study continued, there was good evidence that there would be a substantial improvement in the balance of payments deficit in a few years. The Brookings Institute study provided Congress with all the arguments it needed to let the interest-equalization tax recommendation die in committee.[32]

Foreign aid was the other area of international economic policy where Kennedy faced problems. The central focus of the debate, much of it partisan in tone, was the size of the appropriation. Kennedy originally requested $4.9 billion in January of 1963 and then reduced his request to $4.5 billion in April.[33] The reduction, however, did not satisfy Congress, which ultimately passed an "authorization" bill 34 percent lower than Kennedy's April request.[34] In addition to the general hostility of taxpayers toward foreign aid, Kennedy's request faced stiff opposition in Congress because a special commission studying the matter equivocated in its endorsement of foreign aid, suggesting the United States was trying to do too much for too many.[35] In this political climate, many in Congress expected the corporate community to assume a larger role in meeting the goals of "international development." They felt that not only should America's investment guarantee program be expanded, but nations that were recipients of foreign aid should be urged to offer investment guarantees to foreign corporations—American and otherwise—wishing to invest in their countries, a move that would signal the determination of these nations to make their countries more attractive to American investors.[36]

The final bill broadened and strengthened the so-called Hickenlooper Amendment of 1961, which cut off aid to countries that expropriated American property. The call for greater involvement by private enterprise was not matched by a significant expansion in the investment guarantee program. Little wonder that the business community virtually ignored this request to assume a more prominent role in the development of the Third World.

Like so many other foreign aid bills, this one also generated another committee to study foreign aid—the Advisory Committee on Private Enterprise in Foreign Aid. It proved to be of particular interest to the business community because it was specifically charged with the responsibility of making recommendations "for achieving the most effective utilization of the private enterprise provisions of the [Foreign Aid] Act."[37]

Before the bill or the committee that was to be created under it came into being, President Kennedy was assassinated, paralyzing the nation with grief and disbelief. Bickering over an interest equalization tax or foreign aid seemed utterly trivial when measured against this tragedy.

If John F. Kennedy, the son of millionaire businessman Joseph P. Kennedy, exuded style and charisma, his successor, Lyndon Baines Johnson, the son of a local politician, exhibited all the insecurities of one who desperately wanted the intellectual and cultural advantages that Kennedy had taken for granted. His style did not endear him to the business community, and his message was aimed at a different constituency, those at the bottom of the economic ladder, whose very presence in society blemished his romanticized image of America. Not since Truman had there been such a worrisome figure in the Oval Office, even though influential segments of the business community had come to know Johnson as a result of his long House and Senate careers; he had, after all, been around Washington longer than most of them had.[38]

With respect to international economic problems, the strongest link between the Kennedy and Johnson administrations was the balance of payments issue. It was a problem Johnson dared not ignore, and one that might well signal his attitude toward direct foreign investment and, by implication, the multinational corporation. The only major proposal that was a carry-over from the Kennedy administration was the interest equalization tax. Johnson made it a part of his policy when he urged its passage in his State of the Union message in January, 1964, a request that Congress chose not to implement until August.[39] At most, his endorsement signaled the same desperation over the balance of payments deficit that was revealed during the Kennedy presidency. And there was nothing further to give the business community a reading as to the direction of his thinking.

In the meantime there were problems at home and abroad that drew attention away from the many seamless international economic issues. Johnson had launched a thirteen-point domestic program that he characterized as an unconditional war on poverty. It came as racial tensions, particularly in the South, signaled an even more fundamental social problem than was encompassed by the numerous economic inequalities Johnson was addressing. And on the international front, the United States' slowly escalating involvement in the war between North and South Vietnam was beginning to become the subject of serious public apprehension. In the fall of 1964, it became an even more sensitive issue when the conservative Republican candidate for President, Senator Barry Goldwater of Arizona, tried to make Johnson's reluctant involvement look like a formula for defeat. It was an issue that would ultimately undermine Johnson's immense popularity only months after his landslide victory over Goldwater. He allowed his administration to become hopelessly involved in a major military conflict without fully appreciating the enormous human, economic, or geopolitical consequences of his actions.[40]

The business community did not get a clear reading of Johnson's intentions with regard to foreign economic policy until February, 1965, when he sent his first balance of payments message to Congress.[41] In principle, it was the same problem that Eisenhower and Kennedy had faced, exacerbated by heavy capital outflows in the last few months of 1964[42] because of a combination of foreign demand for American capital and an increase in direct foreign investment by the American business community. He advanced a ten-point program that, when addressing the balance of payments issue, displayed a determination to work with the business and banking communities to achieve his objectives. The President's policies were a mixture of executive initiatives, legislative proposals, and public pressure on American businessmen to refocus their foreign investment policy.

Johnson scheduled a White House conference for February 19, 1964, nine days after his message to Congress, inviting 370 leading executives from the business and banking communities to meet with him, his new Secretary of Commerce John T. Connor, and Federal Reserve Governor J. L. Robertson. The purpose of the conference was to discuss voluntary methods of controlling both short-term corporate lending and direct investment abroad. The banking community was asked to reduce all new overseas loans from the 1964 total of $2 billion to no more than $5 million. The business community was asked to finance all expansion of their foreign subsidiaries from European capital markets rather than draw funds from America's financial institutions. Secretary Connor told the group that the 400 to 500 businesses with overseas investments of $10 million or more would be asked to enlarge their own individual corporate balance of payments surpluses by 15 to 20 percent. Further, these companies would be asked to file quarterly reports with his department describing the steps that had been taken to "achieve the improvements indicated and the reasons for the short fall if any." Although no one had ever said the multinational corporation was the cause of our balance of payments problems, and the quarterly figures generated by the Commerce Department absolved multinational enterprises, Johnson was determined to make them a more visible part of the solution than any of his predecessors had done. Technically speaking, it was not a deliberate attempt to curtail foreign investments, but it was a fairly explicit effort to repatriate a sizable percentage of corporate profits back to the United States and to finance further foreign expansion from European rather than American capital markets. Nothing was said about what would be done if the business or banking communities failed to cooperate with these voluntary measures.[43]

The second phase of the President's program encompassed four measures he requested be given immediate attention by Congress. First, there was a two-year extension of the interest-equalization tax with a broadening of the types of transactions covered so that short- as well as long-term loans negotiated in the U.S. capital markets would be more expensive than loans obtained in foreign capital markets. Second, he asked Congress to give domestic banks the authority to pay a higher interest rate on the time deposits (short-term investments) of foreign governments in U.S. banks than they paid on domestic deposits. This, of course, was intended to encourage foreign governments and monetary authorities to maintain substantial dollar accounts in the United States rather than convert them to gold or transfer them to other financial centers. Third, he asked Congress to approve a measure exempting all U.S. banks, investment bankers, pension funds, and charitable foundations from antitrust laws when they were involved in cooperative agreements among themselves to reduce the balance of payments deficit by curtailing the flow of private dollars and credit from the United States to foreign countries. The action, if approved, would allow the legalization of a whole spectrum of financial arrangements, if they demonstrably improved the balance of payments profile. And finally, and least significant, he requested there be a ceiling on the value of foreign goods that American tourists could bring home duty-free. Congress moved quickly to implement his requests, and the final bill to be approved, the two-year extension of the interest equalization tax, reached Johnson's desk in mid-September. He did not get everything he wanted; yet, it did represent a fairly ambitious legislative initiative that was implemented in a little over seven months.[44]

The third phase of Johnson's balance of payments policy involved the various unilateral actions taken by the executive branch such as a "See the U.S.A." program to encourage foreign tourism and the issuing of executive orders to the appropriate agencies to cut all overseas expenses "to the bone."[45]

Collectively, these policies constituted a frontal assault on the balance of payments deficit, designed to bring about a rapid correction of the disequilibrium. Commerce Department figures to the contrary,[46] the foreign investment patterns of American businesses were perceived as a part of the problem and therefore expected to be a part of the solution. This was the perception of the executive branch of government, which Congress by their actions seemingly endorsed. Even the corporate community did not see it as an unusual series of developments in American economic policy. Perhaps the fact that most of the measures were temporary may have contributed to the routine implementation of the proposals. Whatever the reason, a body of legislation that had the thrust of an "industrial policy" hardly caused a ripple in Washington. The business community was more concerned about the inflationary tendencies in the booming domestic economy than the balance of payments deficit.[47]

The 1965 foreign aid "authorization" bill generated the usual confrontation between supporters and critics of foreign aid, but it focused more on the structure and future of the program than on the dollar amounts authorized. Many of the changes involved an expansion in the technical aspects of the investment guarantee program, particularly as it applied to various forms of private investment in Latin America.[48]

In the midst of the debate, the Advisory Committee on Private Enterprise in Foreign Aid, created during the final months of the Kennedy presidency, delivered its long-awaited report. Authorized by the Foreign Assistance Act of 1963, the nine member group headed by Arthur K. Watson, chairman of IBM, was the first committee ever created to address directly the question of private foreign investments as a parallel component of foreign aid. Watson's letter of transmittal accompanying the report tried to put a new perspective on the foreign aid program:

No matter how carefully our aid dollar is invested ... there still is not enough money nor people to accomplish the vast task the U.S. has undertaken. Two billion dollars annually into the economies of 72 countries is nothing more than $1.44 per person.

It is this realization [the report itself observed], more than the original mandate of the Committee, which finally leads us to urge that the Agency for International Development put increasing stress on its role as catalyst and energizer for private effort. It is only through private resources, our own and those of developing countries themselves, where the additional resources are potentially adequate to meet the challenge.[49]

Rather than fulfill its mandate, the report, in effect, chose to explore methods for "harnessing the vast nongovernmental sector of the United States to the task of accelerating economic growth in the less-developed countries." To further complicate the issue, the Watson committee defined private enterprise in sociological rather than economic terms, involving "business enterprise, labor unions, professional societies and all the rest." The only extended reference to business *per se* came in a discussion of the investment "climate" in the Third World. U.S. business was accustomed to evaluating and accepting normal business risks, the report observed, but not many corporate executives were accustomed to evaluating and accepting political instability, expropriation, discriminatory regulation, or rapid inflation. Faced with these uncertainties, corporate executives instinctively turned elsewhere, where the "climate" was more favorable. Therefore, it was imperative that the investment "climate" be improved. The committee acknowledged that the Agency for International Development (AID) had been doing that with some success but believed it should select a number of "key AID-receiving countries" for "intensive study of factors which may improve the investment climate." The report then undercut its principal recommendation by observing that the committee "is aware of the limits in AID's capacity to use the foreign aid program as leverage to promote private investment or to change the climate."[50]

The foreign aid debate had begun in January, 1965, with Johnson's request for $3.4 billion in funds; it ended in October with Johnson signing a $3.2 billion "appropriation" bill. The Watson Committee report was released in July, seemingly without having the slightest impact on the issue between July and October of 1965 or arousing much interest in the business community. And the United States still had no deliberately supportive foreign investment policy for the American business community, the Watson Committee having, in effect, side-stepped the issue.

By the end of 1965, the balance of payments issue had lost its urgency. The Commerce Department was generating figures that showed a substantial improvement in the balance of payments deficit, suggesting that the voluntary program that Johnson had urged on the business and banking communities the previous February was beginning to show results. It seems the banking community entered more fully into the spirit of the Johnson program than the business community. However real the benefits, Johnson felt the voluntary program was worth continuing and asked both groups to continue to function under its guidelines through 1966, predicting that another good year would move U.S. accounts into equilibrium, i.e., a deficit or surplus of no more than $250 million.[51]

In the meantime, the administration forwarded to Congress a new measure. The measure, known as House bill HR 13103, represented the first deliberate effort to devise a "host" investment policy for foreign corporations wishing to buy into an American business or establish their own subsidiary in the United States. In effect, it addressed the balance of payments question from the opposite direction by making the United States a more attractive area for foreign investments through the elimination of the most obvious discriminatory provisions of existing U.S. tax law. The bill that finally emerged from Congress lowered the rate of taxation on the income earned by foreign investors from 70 percent for individuals and 48 percent for corporations to a flat 30 percent. This was not exactly what the administration intended, but it was not inconsistent with the President's basic objectives. It was considered a part of the administration's long range program to combat the seemingly perpetual balance of payments deficit.[52]

As 1967 drew to a close, it became evident that the balance of payments issue had not been resolved. The deficit would be larger than expected—$3.5 billion as opposed to $1.3 billion for the previous year.[53] The reasons were not hard to find: the U.S. trade surplus was less than it had been in recent years because Europe was buying less; the cost of the war in Vietnam was escalating; there was an increase in U.S. travel abroad; the British pound was devalued; and finally, there was a significant increase in private overseas investments and loans. Several of these factors were outside the control of the administration. The cost of the war in Vietnam, for example, was technically irreversible since the needs of the military could not be cut merely because of a larger deficit in the balance of payments profile. However, the area of private loans and investments could be addressed immediately and decisively.

On January 1, 1968, Johnson's new Secretary of Commerce, Alexander Trowbridge, told a Washington news conference that, for the first time in American history, "mandatory controls" were being established on U.S. private investments abroad. At any time it would be headline-making news, but on New Year's Day, with Congress in recess and government agencies closed, it got maximum exposure. It was deliberately characterized as the "centerpiece" of Johnson's third major effort to correct the balance of payments deficit. Strictly speaking, Johnson's two previous efforts at voluntary controls had not really failed, rather other factors had intervened that made them inadequate remedies in 1968.

Utilizing authority granted the President under an emergency banking act passed in 1940 after war broke out in Europe, individuals or companies that had a 10 percent interest in a foreign business were obliged to conform to the following regulations: during 1968, all new investments in the "developed" countries were either prohibited or limited to a percentage of the 1965–1966 average of investments, and new investments in "developing" countries were limited to 110 percent of the 1965–1966 average of investments. A violation of these "controls" could lead to possible prosecution and a maximum fine of $10,000. In addition to the above, the administration sought to increase American exports and to reverse the pattern of tourism by a combination of discouraging American travel abroad for at least the next two years while encouraging foreign tourism in the United States.[54]

In March of 1968, Johnson surprised the nation by announcing that he would neither seek nor accept the Democratic Party's nomination for the presidency in 1968. This decision, tied to a new initiative to end the Vietnam war, left him with few options in either domestic or foreign economic policy. In the latter area he had already suffered a setback in his 1967 foreign aid bill and he would suffer a further setback during 1968 when Congress passed the smallest foreign aid bill in the twenty-one year history of the program.[55] Furthermore, a trade expansionist act recommended in May of 1968 failed to secure congressional approval and a general recommendation to expand East-West trade, long restricted by the Mutual Defense Assistance

Control Act of 1951 and the Mutual Security Act of 1954, generated nothing more than extensive House and Senate committee hearings.[56] In both instances, Congress and the executive were confronted with strong protectionist sentiments, a viable force since the so-called Kennedy Round of trade negotiations had significantly lowered tariffs on a broad range of products.[57] What made this protectionist sentiment of 1968 so significant was the unexpected support the protectionist groups received from organized labor.

Labor's rank and file had always been more conservative on tariff and trade policy than its leadership. Johnson's trade expansionist proposal in May caused some labor leaders to reexamine their position and to argue that since the Kennedy Round of tariff cuts went into effect, labor was losing jobs as a result of foreign competition from cheap-labor countries. One facet of this complaint was directed against American companies that had become multinational by transferring their labor-intensive operations to cheap-labor markets in the Third World and then importing the finished product back into the United States. It was the first evidence that labor, long a supporter of multinational corporations as a means of spreading democracy and the free enterprise system, was questioning the ultimate effect of corporate multinationalization on our domestic economy. It was also the first indication that the government's assistance programs to domestic industries and workers hurt by the more liberal U.S. trade policy was not providing adequate relief to those sectors of the labor market directly affected. Most labor union officials still saw the American multinational corporation as an accepted instrument of American influence in both the "developed" and "underdeveloped" areas of the world. It was a premise not shared by the rank and file, many of whom saw their jobs being exported.[58]

In the meantime, most of the administration's legislative proposals for mandatory controls on U.S. private investments abroad were rejected by Congress either because they were politically unpopular or because the quarterly figures on the balance of payments profile in 1968 seemed to have turned around again and were significantly better than the 1967 figures, making the President's proposals less urgent. In September, 1968, the President's efforts were further discredited when his former Secretary of Commerce, John T. Connor, characterized the administration's balance of payments policy as a complete failure and called for a quick end to government controls over private foreign investments. The U.S. Chamber of Commerce and the National Association of Manufacturers, in effect, supported

Connor's assessment by issuing statements criticizing the controls. A bipartisan resolution signed by thirty-one members of the House also called for an end to controls. It climaxed several months of negative reaction to Johnson's policies.[59] In his last economic report to Congress in January of 1969, Johnson briefly observed that the temporary program to restrict capital outflows had worked well in 1968 but that it should be ended as soon as possible—when other factors would bring the balance of payments profile into equilibrium.[60]

As the decade of the '60s was drawing to a close, the government's policy toward the multinational corporation was as tangled and as haphazard as it had been when John F. Kennedy confidently stepped forward to lead the country eight years earlier. Two presidents had grappled with foreign economic issues of some urgency without ever devising a clear policy toward multinational enterprises and, it should be said, without ever being pressured to do so—by either the advocates or the critics of the multinationalization process. A corporate entity that was just there in 1960 had become a very visible presence by 1968. The '60s had produced a muddled record of government-business relations, relations that seemed to require continual refocusing with each new issue. What was missing was an international economic policy that took cognizance of the multinational corporation.

NOTES

1. Jim F. Heath, *John F. Kennedy and the Business Community* (Chicago: University of Chicago Press, 1969), pp. 110–111, 127–128.

2. Mira Wilkins, *The Maturing of Multinational Enterprise: American Business Abroad from 1914 to 1970* (Cambridge: Harvard University Press, 1974), pp. 354–361.

3. *Congressional Quarterly Almanac, 1961*, pp. 866–869, quote on p. 868 (henceforth cited as *CQA*).

4. Marina von Neumann Whitman, *Government Risk-Sharing in Foreign Investment* (Princeton: Princeton University Press, 1965), pp. 35–37. What Kennedy was inaugurating ultimately came to be labeled "geographical selectivity."

5. Conveniently summarized in *CQA, 1961*, pp. 332–334.

6. Nonconvertibility refers to losses resulting from the inability of a business to convert assets into a currency equal in value to the assets themselves.

7. *CQA, 1961*, pp. 297–298 for message and provisions of the administration bill.

8. Ibid., p. 298.

9. Ibid., pp. 298–301, 305–306.

10. Ibid., p. 299.

11. Ibid.

12. Ibid., pp. 300–305.

13. Ibid., p. 305.

14. Ibid., pp. 293, 309.

15. Ibid., p. 309.

16. The final bill allowed the President to guarantee up to $1 billion in overseas development investments against all categories of risk. It also authorized the President to guarantee up to 75 percent of an overseas investment (up to $10 million) against unspecified risks. The law also established a unified agency to handle foreign aid. It was known as the Agency for International Development (AID) (Public Law 87-195).

The effectiveness of this agency will figure prominently in subsequent efforts to revise or refocus the foreign aid program in conjunction with private foreign investments.

17. The Arab boycott of firms doing business with Israel was of considerable concern to the international business community. See "Coping with the Arab Boycott of Israel," *Management Monographs, No. 19* (New York: Business International Corporation, 1964) [typescript, not paginated consecutively].

18. *CQA, 1962*, pp. 481–482.

19. *Economic Report of the President... , 1962* (Washington: G.P.O., 1962), pp. 1–27 [President's own statement], quotes on pp. 10, 14 (emphasis added).

20. Most conveniently reprinted in *CQA, 1962*, pp. 879–883.

21. Ibid., pp. 491–496.

22. Ibid., pp. 266–272, 280–282, 291–294.

23. Lobbying positions are summarized in ibid., pp. 221–294.

24. Arthur S. Link and William B. Catton, *American Epoch: A History of the United States since the 1890's,* 2nd ed. rev. (New York: Alfred A. Knopf, 1963), p. 868.

25. *CQA, 1962*, pp. 479–509.

26. Ibid., p. 509.

27. Ibid., pp. 301–304.

28. William H. Chafe, *The Unfinished Journey: America Since World War II* (New York: Oxford University Press, 1986), pp. 208–217.

29. *Economic Report of the President... , 1963* (Washington: G.P.O., 1963), pp. i–xxviii [President's own statement], quote on p. 101.

30. The President's special message is conveniently reprinted in *CQA, 1963*, pp. 996–1000.

31. The "capital accounts" deficit is the amount by which the outward flow of capital from a country exceeds the inward flow. It addressed the dramatic increase in the sale of foreign securities in the United States. Kennedy referred to it as a "flood" (ibid., p. 998).

32. Ibid., pp. 586–588, summary of the Brookings Institute study; ibid., p. 585.

33. Ibid., p. 265. The President's message of April 2, with the request for the lesser amount, is printed in full in ibid., pp. 983–987.

34. Ibid., p. 288.

35. This was the Clay Commission, headed by retired General Lucius D. Clay, one of America's most respected generals in World War II. Because a sizeable number of businessmen were on the commission, it was expected that the

commission's findings would provide the administration with the kind of ammunition needed to win Congressional support for substantial foreign aid funds. The fact that the commission report equivocated only served to provide additional ammunition to the growing number of foreign aid critics (ibid., p. 257).

36. Ibid., pp. 258, 259, 262, 270, 271, 273.

37. David A. Baldwin, ed., *Foreign Aid and American Foreign Policy: A Documentary Analysis* (New York: Frederick A. Praeger, 1966), p. 158.

38. For a critical study of Johnson's background see Robert Caro, *The Years of Lyndon Johnson: The Path to Power* (New York: Alfred A. Knopf, 1982), I. For a more sympathetic treatment see Doris Kearns, *Lyndon Johnson and the American Dream* (New York: Harper & Row, 1976).

39. *CQA, 1964*, p. 545.

40. William H. Chafe, *The Unfinished Journey*, pp. 228–243, 273–301 for a convenient, if not detached, account of the events summarized in this paragraph.

41. Message conveniently reprinted in *CQA, 1965*, pp. 1390–1393.

42. The Commerce Department reported that, "All components of private capital outflows except purchases of foreign securities moved upward last year [1964]: Direct investments were up $0.4 billion to $2.4 billion; net lending by banks (including assets held for customers) rose by about $1.0 billion to $2.5 billion."

This special report, published in September, 1965, was a reflection of the administration's growing concern that foreign investments were a "major feature" [p. 22] in the balance of payments problem.

For a detailed analysis see U.S. Department of Commerce, "Foreign Investments, 1964–65," *Survey of Current Business, 1965* (Washington: G.P.O., 1965), No. 9, Sept. 1965, pp. 22–32, quotes on p. 22.

43. *CQA, 1965*, p. 867.

The Commerce Department's study cited in note 42 states "Capital outflows for direct investment abroad have been moving up to successively higher rates since the end of World War II. They reached $2.4 billion in 1964 and have shown a further increase so far this year [1965]. *At the same time the increased income derived from foreign affiliates has been one of the major elements of strength in the balance of payments.*"

"Foreign Investments, 1964–65," *Survey of Current Business, 1965*, No. 9, Sept. 1965, pp. 22–23 (emphasis added).

44. *CQA, 1965*, p. 867.

45. Ibid.

46. See note 42.

47. It is worth noting that Kim McQuaid's careful study of the Business Council makes no reference to the Council trying to influence Johnson's efforts to correct the balance of payment problem. See *Big Business and Presidential Power: From FDR to Reagan* (New York: William Morrow & Co. Inc., 1982), pp. 223–257.

48. *CQA, 1965*, pp. 422–423. The measure was signed into law on September 6 (Public Law 89-171).

49. The Watson committee report and his letter of transmittal are printed in Baldwin, ed., *Foreign Aid and American Foreign Policy*, pp. 158–171, quoted material on pp. 158, 170–171.

50. Ibid., pp. 170–171.

51. *Economic Report of the President…, 1966* (Washington: G.P.O., 1966), pp. 15 [President's own statement], 160, 165–167, 189.

52. *CQA, 1966*, pp. 732–735.

It should be noted that when the Senate Finance Committee and the Senate itself finished with House bill HR 13103, it had dozens of irrelevant riders that provided for everything from financing presidential elections with federal revenues to a provision reducing the excise taxes on hearses. The original intent of the bill was hopelessly obscured by the more newsworthy riders and the techniques used to attach them to the original bill. The sarcastically dubbed "Christmas-tree" bill triggered a host of critical articles on the manipulatory tactics of lobbyists with little or no attention to those sections of the bill that represented the first efforts at formulating a "host" country investment policy. Johnson signed the so-called "foreign investors tax law" with some reluctance, endorsing only the foreign investment provisions of the bill and the much publicized presidential campaign finance rider. Because House bill HR 13103 had inadvertently become the last bill of the session to alter the Internal Revenue Code, it became an example of the worst features of the legislative process, precluding a thorough airing of the rationale behind this first attempt at devising an investment policy for foreign multinationals *in* the United States (ibid., pp. 732–740).

53. Ibid., *1968*, p. 718.

54. Ibid., pp. 717–719.

The measure also stated that companies lacking an historical record of foreign investments during the 1965–1966 base year were simply barred from all foreign investments during 1968. Further, foreign direct investors were expected to repatriate either the same percentage of their share of earnings as they repatriated during 1964–1965 or their share of earnings that exceeded the limit set for a new investment, whichever was greater (ibid., p. 718).

55. *CQA, 1967*, pp. 679–683, 698–704; ibid., *1968*, pp. 419–433, 604–608.

56. Ibid., pp. 729–734, 735–736.

57. In the second half of 1967 and then again in 1968 there were aggressive lobbying efforts by several major sectors of the business community to neutralize or scuttle many of the tariff cuts that had been agreed upon in multilateral negotiations following the passage of President Kennedy's Trade Expansion Act of 1962. The three years of negotiations, known as the Kennedy Round, were the most ambitious effort to date at trade liberalization on a global scale. The results of these negotiations triggered a wave of protectionist lobbying from steel, cotton textiles, chemicals, and agricultural interests that severely tested the Johnson administration's political influence in Congress. (Ibid., *1967*, pp. 805–820 and ibid., *1968*, pp. 729–734.)

Technically speaking this political infighting had no direct bearing on America's foreign investments except insofar as any effort to neutralize or undermine the meticulously negotiated tariff schedules could well make the members of the European Economic Community less receptive to further American investments within its carefully defined market.

The protectionist effort failed, but the experience put corporate lobbyists in the forefront of the legislative process. The disadvantages of being in the public eye were more than offset by the contacts and associations that flowed from this common effort, even if it failed to produce the desired results.

58. C. Fred Bergsten, Thomas Horst, and Theodore H. Moran, *American Multinationals and American Interests* (Washington: The Brookings Institution, 1978), pp. 99–100, 111; *CQA, 1976*, pp. 816–817; and Robert A. Pastor, *Congress*

and the Politics of U.S. Foreign Economic Policy, 1929–1976 (Berkeley: University of California Press, 1980), pp. 131–132.

59. Ibid., p. 717.

Fourteen more months would pass before a Republican administration removed Johnson's mandatory controls. During these fourteen months, escalating racial violence, a deteriorating military situation in Vietnam, and the Soviet invasion of Czechoslovakia made our balance of payments problems seem almost trivial by comparison.

60. *Economic Report of the President..., 1969* (Washington: G.P.O., 1969), pp. 15–16 [President's own statement].

5 EMERGENCE OF AN INTERNATIONAL ECONOMIC POLICY: 1968–1973

Probably not since Reconstruction has America displayed the querulousness that marked the late '60s and early '70s.[1] The country's greatness was being devalued nightly on network news as reports from Vietnam documented in gruesome detail our military frustrations. In a matter of months President Nixon discovered that he had lost much of the good will that the country normally accords a newly elected president.

The ever-increasing trade deficit of the late '60s and the growing congressional hostility to foreign aid seemed to signal the end to what had come to be characterized as the largess of America's postwar international policy. The rebuilding of the war-torn countries of Europe had been completed and those we had attempted to save from Communism by a massive infusion of foreign aid and hesitant American corporate investments had become our competitors during the late '60s. The world had become smaller and the United States was no longer the dominant force, the provider, or the architect.

Nixon and his advisors sensed the change and proclaimed a new international economic policy, a policy presumably more consistent with America's limited resources and the fact that our previous role, however defined, was no longer appropriate. Nixon would argue that we must shape our global economic policy not through our largess but through geopolitical statecraft, fashioned out of what we perceived to be our global imperatives. With the myth of invincibility shattered, America's international economic policy had to be nimble rather than rigid, sensitive to the criticisms of domestic as well as foreign interests.[2] In such a climate the multinational corporation no longer had a defined or guaranteed role, but neither—it should be recognized—did any other segment of American society. If the late '60s were any index, the times seemed ripe for a massive brawl that would leave all parties bruised and alienated from one another.

Nixon's election to the presidency gave the Republican Party its first opportunity to reshape American foreign economic policy in almost a decade. But in truth, there were no fundamental differences between the two parties in this area of policy making, both being aware of America's obligation to foster a global economy, at least for the free world. The only policy of the Johnson administration destined for immediate change was the mandatory restrictions on U.S. private investments abroad.[3] Before the Nixon administration had a chance to address this issue, however, the Democrat-controlled House Foreign Affairs Committee authorized its Subcommittee on Foreign Economic Policy to hold hearings on several resolutions calling for the immediate termination of controls on U.S. foreign direct investments.[4]

These hearings, held between March 26 and May 1, 1969, generated some interesting testimony from the private as well as the public sectors. Spokesmen for the Manufacturing Chemists Association, Occidental Petroleum Corporation, the United Fruit Company, the Associated General Contractors of America, the Committee for a National Trade Policy, the National Association of Manufacturers, and the U.S. Chamber of Commerce spoke out against controls. After the President's announcement of April 4, 1969, that he intended to "relax controls," individuals testifying before the subcommittee took pains to point out that Nixon's statement had not gone far enough, citing the hardships flowing from the controls or focusing on the fact that the controls, in place since 1965 or 1968, had not—and never would—correct the balance of payments deficit.[5]

The only significant testimony in support of continued controls came on May 1, the last day of the hearings. Andrew J. Biemiller, director of the AFL-CIO department of legislation, set forth organized labor's position. If there were administrative problems associated with the maintenance of controls, the solution, Biemiller argued, was to correct the problem, not eliminate the controls. The government should have the authority to regulate large outflows of capital to foreign countries because such authority was "essential to the well-being of the American people."[6]

Nixon's announcement on April 4, and the subsequent revision of procedures in the Commerce Department's program of restrictions on foreign investments, immediately lessened the concerns of the business community. On May 1 the hearings ended and no further action was taken on the resolutions calling for the termination of controls.

Less than two months after his April 4th announcement, Nixon sent his first foreign aid message to Congress. It was not the usual plea to adequately finance a global assistance program—an idea that had long since lost its cosmopolitan glamour. A General Advisory Committee on Foreign Assistance Programs had recommended the creation of an Overseas Private Investment Corporation (OPIC) to take over the investment guarantee and investment promotion functions of the Agency for International Development (AID). Nixon made it the centerpiece of his approach to foreign assistance:

> The purpose of the [Overseas Private Investment] Corporation is to provide businesslike management of investment incentives *now in our laws* so as to contribute to the economic and social progress of developing nations. . . .
>
> Venture capital seeks profits, not adventure. To guide this capital to high-risk areas, the Federal Government presently offers a system of insurance and guarantees. Like the Federal Housing Administration in the housing field here at home, the Overseas Private Investment Corporation will be able to place the credit of the United States government behind the insurance and guarantees which the Corporation would sell to U.S. private investors.
>
> The Corporation will . . . carry out investment survey and development activities. And it will undertake for AID some of the technical assistance required to strengthen private enterprise abroad.

Additionally, he urged an expanded emphasis on technical assistance and the channeling of assistance through international development banks so that other economically advanced nations could share in the burden of international economic development in the Third World. There would also be a greater emphasis on food production to eliminate starvation and malnutrition and an emphasis on family planning to curtail population growth in underdeveloped areas that could not sustain an ever-increasing population. In each of these endeavors there was a clear reference to private firms or private investments being in some way related to their implementation.[7]

Some of this emphasis has to be attributed to the fact that each succeeding foreign aid bill faced stiffer congressional scrutiny than the previous bill. By 1969, many members of Congress were openly hostile to the whole concept of foreign aid, and their constituents agreed.[8] Yet, the Nixon administration seemed to be signaling its desire to see the private sector, either through loans (multinational banks) or direct investments (multinational corporations), play a larger role in improving the lot of the Third World. The concept of private sector initiatives had been a part of the strategy of previous administrations, although perhaps a less prominent part of their legislative package.

A compromise foreign aid "authorization" bill did not secure House and Senate approval until December 19, 1969, literally days before the end of the congressional session. In the process, the provisions for OPIC were dropped by the Senate Foreign Relations Committee because the committee's chairman, J. William Fulbright of Arkansas, was challenging the whole idea of foreign aid. The OPIC provisions were put back into the bill on the Senate floor through an amendment offered by Senator Jacob Javits of New York, a long-time advocate of private investments in underdeveloped countries. But the whole issue was left unresolved when this congressional session ended without Congress being able to agree on a foreign aid "appropriation" bill to provide the funds needed to implement the just-passed "authorization" bill.[9]

The "authorization" bill, Nixon's first foreign aid measure, proved to be the smallest in the history of the foreign aid program to date. OPIC, the new investment insurance and guarantee program and the distinctive feature of this administration's approach to foreign aid, failed to secure broad support as a result of the mounting hostility to all forms of foreign aid. In fact, the "appropriation" bill to fund the "authorization" bill, with the OPIC provision included, would not be passed until the next session of Congress. And even then OPIC's future was uncertain for several weeks because of an intense debate over two controversial items in the previously passed "authorization" bill, i.e., a $50 million authorization for military aid to South Korea and a $54.5 million authorization for Phantom jets for the Chinese government on the island of Taiwan. By the time the foreign aid "appropriation" bill reached the President's desk, the sum for OPIC had been reduced to $37.5 million, half of what the President had originally requested.[10]

In the eight months that had elapsed since the President sent his first foreign aid message to Congress, with the OPIC proposal included, the business community remained strangely aloof. Token statements were made to be sure, but corporate America sent no clear message of support for the new agency. Foreign aid was growing more unpopular with each passing week and the OPIC idea, whatever its potential significance, was too closely identified with a program that had not only lost the glamour of unselfish generosity, but for many, its fundamental validity.

Shortly before the end of the year, Nixon outlined his trade policy for Congress, obviously of great interest to the corporate community. He characterized it as a blueprint for the '70s, when trade problems would differ significantly from those of the '50s and '60s. Apart from the expected request for authority to further reduce tariffs, eliminate the remaining nontariff barriers, and offer additional aid for industries and their employees affected by lower tariff schedules, there was a different tone to this trade policy message.

Nixon avoided the lofty rhetoric of Kennedy and the honest platitudes of Johnson, but he did not disguise his perception of the climate within which America would have to function in the next decade:

. . . world economic interdependence has become a fact. Reductions in tariffs and in transportation costs have internationalized the world economy just as satellites and global television have internationalized the world communications network. The growth of the multinational corporation provides a dramatic example of this development.

[Therefore] We must take into account the far-reaching changes which have occurred in investment abroad and in patterns of world trade.

We can no longer afford to think of our trade policies in the old, simple terms of liberalism vs. protectionism. Rather we must learn to treat investment, production, employment and trade as interrelated and interdependent.[11]

Nixon had no idea of the prophetic import of his words when he transmitted this message to Congress.

The President next undertook a sweeping review of U.S. foreign policy in a massively detailed message to Congress on February 18, 1970. While it seemed to presume a partnership between the Federal government and the multinational corporation, at least to the extent that the President suggested that his administration would like to see the private sector do more to improve the lot of the underdeveloped countries of the world, it also repeated the themes that lie behind the

OPIC proposal advanced in his first foreign aid message to Congress in 1969. Furthermore, he announced his intention to establish a Commission on International Trade and Investment Policy and then explicitly tied American investment policy to trade:

Foreign investment, symbolized by the multinational corporation, has been increasingly important in relation to the flow of goods which have been the focus of traditional trade policy. We must explore more fully the relationship between our trade and foreign investment policies.[12]

Linking the multinational corporation to trade "policy" rather than to balance of payments "problems" represented a shift in approach from what had been pursued by the two previous administrations.

The hostility of Congress toward continued foreign aid was the most obvious explanation for the shift, but Nixon was also trying to give America's global priorities a different orientation. The "Nixon Doctrine" proclaimed in this policy statement was self-help and partnership, and the explicit message that the United States would no longer assume the role of the world's policeman—or banker. The problem of being "overextended" served to give the partnership theme a high visibility. In theory, at least, the multinational corporation was a part of this partnership.[13]

Several weeks later, on March 8, 1970, the (Rudolph A.) Peterson Task Force that had been appointed by Nixon in September, 1969, to undertake a comprehensive review of the U.S. aid program since World War II presented its findings. Where Nixon had advanced the idea of "partnership," the Peterson Task Force spoke in terms of "cooperative" endeavors. Its principal suggestions respecting the multinational corporation and private investments included a strong endorsement of OPIC, an end to the restrictive provisions of the Hickenlooper Amendment, and the elimination of current restraints on U.S. direct investments in developing countries. Like the President's February 18th message, the proposals of the Peterson Task Force with respect to the multinational corporation, as well as the proposals directly related to reorganizing the whole foreign aid program, got buried in an increasingly bitter debate over the administration's policies in Southeast Asia.[14]

Two developments in the spring of 1970 seriously compromised Nixon's credibility and transformed the Nixon Doctrine into a cliché, at least among his critics. On April 30, Nixon indicated that he intended to order U.S. forces into Cambodia to destroy Communist sanctuaries along the South Vietnam border. At about the same time, details of a clandestine war in Laos became available, proving that the administration was expanding rather than curtailing U.S. involvement in Southeast Asia. It caused many to conclude that the President was not only misleading Congress, but usurping its authority.

The war in Southeast Asia dominated the legislative agenda of the 91st Congress, and it was December 31, 1970, before Congress was able to reach agreement on a drastically reduced foreign aid "appropriation" bill—some 33 percent below the amount originally requested. The OPIC appropriation was cut in half by the House and then restored at the insistence of the Senate.[15]

But the real debate was between the "hawks" and the "doves" over what was happening—or not happening—in Southeast Asia. The multinational corporation figured prominently in the administration's thinking at the beginning of the year, but before the year ended the first signs began to appear that it was losing its privileged status as one of the instruments for bringing developing nations more fully into the global economy.

The first serious critics of the multinational corporation were the staff professionals from the Washington headquarters of several of the larger unions. As early as 1969, Andrew Biemiller, director of the AFL-CIO department of legislation, had spoken out against the removal of controls on private direct foreign investments that had been imposed during the Johnson administration in connection with our seemingly perpetual balance of payments problems.[16] By 1970, labor's attitude toward the multinational corporation had become even more hostile. Traditionally, the rank-and-file of organized labor had been skeptical of corporate multinationalization, freer trade, foreign aid, and all other "give-away" policies of the Federal government. But many of the leaders of the labor movement were willing to view our postwar economic and Cold War problems in a broader perspective—willing to see tangible benefits in the spread of America's free enterprise system throughout the world. With the apparent end of the Cold War, a growing disillusionment with the Southeast Asian policies of the two previous administrations, and the abysmal record of this administration in resolving problems in our domestic economy, the leadership of organized labor began to take aim at multinational corporations in the industrial sector as part of its general displeasure with the Nixon administration.[17]

Nathaniel Goldfinger, director of the department of research of the AFL-CIO, provided the most carefully crafted statement of criticism to date. The occasion was a series of hearings in mid-March by a subcommittee of the Joint Economic Committee of Congress reviewing, in the light of Nixon's February 18th message, America's "foreign economic policy for the 1970s." The specific subject was trade policy toward "developed" countries. Goldfinger appeared on the next to last day of this phase of the subcommittee's hearings, after a string of witnesses from business, academia, and private research organizations had set forth their views as to what America's trade policy should be in the coming decade. None of these witnesses took issue with the basic postwar pattern of multilaterally negotiated treaties that promoted freer trade, and only a few took notice of the operational influence of multinational corporations in their testimony.[18] Goldfinger, on the other hand, was the only witness to describe America's position in world trade as deteriorating, with an adverse impact on American workers, communities, and industries: "A thorough revision of U.S. government posture and policy is required to meet present realities in the world market."[19]

Goldfinger admitted that some of the "new developments," such as the revival of Europe's war-shattered economies and the recent emergence of the European Common Market, were inevitable. But others, he insisted, were traceable to the absence of appropriate Federal restrictions or restraints. Specifically, he cited the skyrocketing rise of foreign investments by U.S. firms and the "rapid spread of multinational corporations." He then systematically itemized the groups that had been adversely affected: "textile and apparel workers," "steel workers," "workers in glass and allied products industries," "shoe workers," "electrical products workers," "workers in several different industries affected by a combination of Mexican and U.S. law which encourages development of labor intensive operations of U.S. companies in Mexican plants," and "the increasing foreign production of films for the movies and TV by foreign companies and U.S.-owned companies." The difficulties these various groups of workers were experiencing were not traceable to the multinationalization process alone, but in every case the multinational corporation was a contributing factor. He continued:

> There is no one-shot panacea or simple collection of a few easy answers. A change in posture and a battery of new policies and mechanisms are needed to make it possible to get at the varied different causes of the specific problems that affect different groups of workers, different product-lines, and different industries.

Further, he called for an end to our "head-in-the-sand-posture" and the continued maintenance of policies that had been developed in the 18th and 19th centuries when England was the "only major industrial nation in the world."[20]

Goldfinger's ability to isolate the specific sectors of the American work force that were being adversely affected suggested his testimony reflected a considerable research effort by the staff of the AFL-CIO. The rhetoric was deliberately intemperate, although it probably should be noted that intemperate rhetoric had become a fact of life in American politics by 1970.

But Goldfinger was not merely summarizing the findings of the Union's research staff; he put into the record the resolutions of the recent annual convention of the AFL-CIO on the subject of inter-national trade. Their 11th resolution dealt specifically with the problem of U.S. multinational corporations:

> The export of U.S. capital and its effect on international trade should be thoroughly investigated and appropriate government supervision and nec-essary regulations should be instituted. Until there is a basic improvement of the balance-of-payments problem, there should be direct restrictions and controls on U.S. investments in developed countries. Mechanisms for such restrictions are already established in all other major industrial countries. Effective tax policies should be adopted to prevent avoidance and/or evasion of U.S. taxation on profits from foreign investments. The Congress should examine the operations of international companies for the purpose of developing supervision and regulations of the operations of U.S.-based multi-national firms.[21]

The multinational corporation was now coming under fire from organized labor at the highest level of its decision making structure. And, although the context of these hearings was trade, Goldfinger was not focusing on America's trade or tariff policy. The multinational corporation in "developed countries" must be controlled by the Federal government with realistic trade, investment, monetary, and tax policies. The topic was specific; the area of remedial action was comprehensive.

Aside from four more days of congressional hearings in July by the same subcommittee of the Joint Economic Committee, there was nothing to suggest that there was either any concerted effort to dis-credit multinational corporations in general or, conversely, to give them a pivotal role in American foreign economic policy. The lack of a common focus in the testimony of sixteen witnesses tended to make the hearings inconclusive save for the fact that organized labor no longer saw any benefits flowing from the multinationalization of American business.[22]

In the confrontational style of the times, corporate America discovered that it was not going to be able to sit on the sidelines and watch the brawl. Blacks, environmentalists, women, antiwar activists, and labor demanded change. Of the various groups challenging the policies and attitudes of the past, multinational corporations were most concerned about the growing criticism of organized labor.

By midyear, the representatives of business also recognized that the climate was changing among many members of Congress. Criticism of Nixon's foreign policy in Southeast Asia, lack of support for foreign aid, and a general distrust of the traditional probusiness bias of any Republican administration all suggested a disturbingly critical climate in the months ahead.

Nixon's September 15, 1970, message to Congress on reorganizing the foreign aid program temporarily diverted attention away from the multinational corporation and suggested that, at the very least, this administration was addressing the foreign aid issue as a drain on the government's resources. He outlined his proposed reforms and promised to forward new foreign aid assistance legislation to Congress early in 1971.[23] The projected six-point reform program was impressive in scope but the climate of distrust was firmly in place and Nixon's plan to reorganize foreign aid was in trouble long before the actual bills were sent to Congress in April of 1971. The repeated confrontations between Blacks and the police in cities throughout the United States, the growing symbolism of the Kent State incident, and the highly publicized forthcoming rally in Washington to protest our continued involvement in the Vietnam war all served to poison the climate for reassessing the foreign aid program.

In the midst of all this, in January, 1971, an increase in our balance of payments deficit prompted the Treasury Department, the Federal Reserve Board, and the Commerce Department to jointly announce a one-year extension of the existing curbs on U.S. private investments and bank lending abroad and to request Congress to renew the interest-equalization tax on foreign security purchases in the United States, which was due to expire in March. It marked a temporary retreat from the administration's announced goals of phasing out all controls restricting capital outflows. The Treasury Department was quite candid, saying the extension was necessary in view of a "serious continuing balance of payments problem."[24]

In May of 1971, the Subcommittee on International Trade of the Senate Finance Committee held its first series of hearings on what the subcommittee came to perceive as a "changing world economic system."[25] The context for this initial set of hearings was provided by the subcommittee's staff report, *A Survey of Current Issues to be Studied by the Subcommittee on International Trade*. It was released three days before the opening of the hearings and focused on numerous interrelated issues that had emerged as a result of the "structural changes" that had evolved over the past twenty years. One of the issues requiring immediate and careful scrutiny was the part played by multinational corporations in this changing world economic system.[26] Eighteen witnesses testified before the subcommittee, including three of the most important figures in the growing debate over the role of the multinational corporation in American economic life— George Meany, president of the AFL-CIO, Orville Freeman, president of Business International, and George Ball, senior managing director of the Lehman Brothers investment firm.[27]

Meany was the first of the three to testify. His testimony left no doubt that American labor was mounting a frontal assault on the multinational corporation. The senior spokesman for American labor declared his opposition to "all phases" of "investment, trade, export technology, and international banking" that affected American labor. "We seek a trade policy that enhances the well-being of the American people in place of one that enhances private greed."[28] He then introduced into the record a statement by the AFL-CIO Executive Council that urged tax measures to remove *any* incentives to foreign investments for production or assembly facilities and to curb the flow of U.S. capital out of the country.[29]

In the deferential questioning that followed, Meany freely admitted that labor's position on overseas investments and expansion had grown "more critical" in recent years. Given the sweeping language of his formal statement to the subcommittee, his matter-of-fact admission of labor's disenchantment with the multinationalization of American business seemed almost anticlimactic.

Ball and Freeman testified on May 19th and 20th respectively. For both men the multinational corporation was a self-evident asset, not only for what it did for America in the international arena, but also for its significant contribution to the health of our domestic economy. Each of them took note of the most obvious objections to the multinational corporation, but their formal statements were positive rather than defensive or apologetic in tone. And they urged the maintenance of a trade policy that was conducive to the continued development of the multinational corporation.[30]

A month later, in July, 1971, the President received his first formal report on global economic policy. The previous year, in May, 1970, Nixon had named twenty-seven of the nation's leading businessmen, labor leaders, and academics to a commission, the Commission on International Trade and Investment Policy. The group was asked to make recommendations that would serve as policy guidelines for the remainder of the '70s. Between May, 1970, and July, 1971, the commission collected the views of nearly one hundred individuals. Their report, plus the two additional volumes of specialized studies that they had requested, seemed to cover every possible international economic policy issue that might confront the country in the '70s.[31]

The basic thesis of the commission's report as released in July, 1971, was that the United States was currently facing a "crisis of confidence"—a belief that the way we had been doing things since the end of World War II would no longer work in the '70s. The intent of the commission's recommendations was to "redress [America's] international economic position," which, they suggested, was far more worrisome than our international political or military position. The report candidly admitted that foreign trade and investment practices had created domestic problems that had to be recognized and addressed. Additionally, there were both immediate and long-term issues that had to be resolved through negotiations with our major trading partners. Foreign investment was identified as a long-term issue, and the commission recommended that the United States "should strive to reduce artificial incentives and impediments to foreign direct investment in *developed* countries." Foreign private investments in *developing* countries were characterized as making "a major contribution to their economic progress."[32]

While the commission took note of the fact that there were critics of the multinational corporation—and even published the papers of some of the harshest critics—it still insisted that the available evidence suggested that the multinationalization of corporate America did not have a negative impact on labor, the transfer of valuable technology, or any of the other problems usually linked with the phenomenon of multinationalization. There was explicit support of OPIC, for this commission a clear example of the kinds of policies that should be pursued in the '70s.[33]

The commission made two specific recommendations. The first was a recommendation that all controls or restraints on U.S. investments abroad be phased out over the next three to five years, "because they were not effective at the time of imposition and have become increasingly more harmful."[34] Organized labor was of course already on record as wanting to see these and other controls expanded. The second recommendation was to make the recently formed (January, 1971) Council on International Economic Policy (CIEP) the principal architect of America's international economic policy. The commission saw what no other study group had previously recognized; namely, that establishing an advisory body to the President to coordinate the administration of a global economic policy at the highest level was at least as important as any of the specifics that had created the "crisis of confidence" that was the theme of their report.[35]

In August, 1971, Nixon's new economic policy unexpectedly and dramatically captured center stage when he announced that he was severing the link between the dollar and gold, allowing the dollar to "float" on the international market. He also imposed a 10 percent surcharge on imports. The domestic side of this major shift in our economic policy was an announced ninety-day freeze on prices, wages, and rents to counteract the inflationary forces in the economy. For a time, the multinational corporation faded from view, except among the technocrats on both sides of the issue. Labor, for example, discovered that in Nixon's "new economic policy" it had a more immediate problem, i.e., the ninety-day freeze on wages with the prospect that it might be extended if the hoped-for improvements in the domestic economy did not materialize.[36]

In September, 1971, Congress took up the Burke-Hartke bill, the first bill ever to come before Congress that was explicitly hostile to the policies and practices of the multinational corporation. The bill proposed to modify the manner in which the foreign income of American multinational corporations would be taxed, and provided for a licensing procedure for all U.S. firms contemplating foreign investments or the export of their technology. The decision to grant or deny a license pivoted on the probable impact the foreign investment or the transfer of technology might have on jobs in the United States. In addition, the bill required an appropriate disclosure of the scope of foreign operations of all U.S. multinational corporations and restricted the imports of these companies to prevent them from using foreign production or assembly facilities to supply their markets in the United States to the detriment of American workers.[37]

The bill, which had been prepared by the AFL-CIO and introduced by Senator Vance Hartke of Indiana and Representative James A. Burke of Massachusetts, was too explicitly hostile toward the multinational corporation for most members of Congress. Consequently, it was promptly rejected, a move that the Nixon administration readily endorsed. Yet, as a sign of organized labor's escalating hostility toward corporate multinationals, it sent a clear message to the Federal government and to the corporate world that organized labor hoped to use the legislative process to rein in America's multinational corporations.

In December, 1971, less than six months after the release of the report by the Commission on International Trade and Investment Policy, Nixon had still another study of the world economy sitting on his desk. Popularly known as the "Peterson Report," it was the work of Peter Peterson, Nixon's Assistant for International Economic Affairs. Peterson initially prepared a draft "report" so that its contents might be reviewed by select members of the administration and by key members of Congress before the formal release of the study. Peterson's staff also revised the "report" even further in the light of several specific studies authorized by the President subsequent to Peterson's initial assignment. The publication of *The United States in a Changing World Economy* in December, 1971, represented the culmination of at least nine months of work by Peterson and his staff.[38] It contained a thorough statistical analysis of U.S. direct investments abroad during the '60s with a section devoted to "the new industrial type—the multinational corporation" and its distinctive characteristics. The section on the multinational corporation concluded with the observation:

> Not enough is known with certainty about the specific economic effects of MNCs [multinational corporations], including their effect on jobs in this country. One thing, however, is already clear. These corporations are a major force in expanding both world trade and America's role in the world economy. Also MNCs are an integral part of our technological and managerial expertise. To seriously restrict the activities of these corporations in their foreign operations would obviously be a major step back from the relatively open and interdependent world we have tried to help build.[39]

This judicious conclusion, following an explicit reference to the serious concerns of America's labor unions, provided the context for a balanced debate over the place of the multinational corporation in America's overall economic development.

But the study by Peter Peterson had virtually no impact on America's foreign economic policy. On March 24, 1972, less than three months after the release of the Peterson study, Senator William Fulbright, the Chairman of the Senate Foreign Relations Committee, announced that his committee would undertake a major inquiry into the "role of the multinational corporation and their [sic] relationship to the foreign policy" of the United States.[40] The context of Fulbright's unexpected announcement was the publication of documents by syndicated columnist Jack Anderson linking ITT with attempts to influence U.S. policy toward Chile in 1970. Anderson's evidence purported to show that ITT attempted to prevent the election of Salvador Allende Gossens to the presidency of Chile and, that failing, to instigate his removal from office by force. The documents further indicated that ITT regularly approached the CIA, the White House, the State Department, and the Justice Department in an effort to have the Federal government support ITT's policies in Chile.[41] As a result of these tactics, many of them involving the personal intervention of Harold Geneen, chairman of ITT, one of the country's most visible multinational corporations suddenly found itself the object of a major congressional investigation.

The Senate Foreign Relations Committee subsequently voted to look beyond this particular case and to undertake a broad investigation of multinational firms in terms of their influence on U.S. foreign policy and the overall impact of their activities on America's domestic economy.[42] To accomplish this task, the Senate Foreign Relations Committee established a Subcommittee on Multinational Corporations, chaired by Senator Frank Church of Idaho. The parent committee further agreed that the hearings of its subcommittee should be postponed until after the elections in November, 1972, to avoid all charges of partisan politics.[43] In the meantime, the climate within which these precedent-making hearings would take place was being provided by another Senate subcommittee.

The Senate Finance Committee's Subcommittee on International Trade had previously assumed a "legislative oversight" role in connection with the foreign economic policies of the United States. As such, on June 1, 1972, it invited "interested parties" to submit factually documented papers covering key issues raised by the activities of "international business organizations," and explicitly solicited comments on all major issues with which the multinational corporation was identified. Some fifteen replies, including one from the AFL-CIO, one from the Center for Multinational Studies, two from the Department of Commerce, and two from the National Foreign Trade Council were submitted. Of all the replies, the Council's studies proved to be the most useful. One focused on trade and the other on proposed changes in the tax code with respect to U.S. investments abroad. In addition, ITT, IBM, and the Varian Corporation each submitted papers on their international operations, as did several other less prominent multinationals, each of them giving a positive description of their foreign business practices and obviously distancing themselves from the kinds of activities with which ITT was identified.[44]

In the meantime, the Nixon administration had been busily engaged in defusing the Vietnam war issue by removing all U.S. ground combat troops from South Vietnam in anticipation of the 1972 presidential election. While Secretary of State Henry Kissinger had been unable to deliver a cease-fire agreement before that election, his efforts had done enough to silence many of the administration's more vocal critics on this issue. In terms of the level of U.S. involvement in Southeast Asia, 1973 was looking much more promising to Republican strategists than 1972 had been.

What did not make the headlines during these weeks of growing concern about the activities of America's multinational corporations was a meeting at New York's exclusive Hotel Pierre on February 1, 1973, to consider "what to do about the attacks on multinational corporations." The meeting had been called by Business International, a New York-based government monitoring organization that served the internationally-oriented corporate community. Attending the meeting were about seventy corporate executives, the "overwhelming number" representing U.S.-based multinational corporations. The group decided to set up a Task Force to discuss with their European and Japanese counterparts the feasibility of establishing a world-wide group of executives to deal with the growing hostility toward multinational corporations. J. L. Hanigan, the CEO of Brunswick Corporation, was selected as chairman of the Task Force and this first meeting set the stage for a concerted effort by business to answer its critics. Another year would pass before this effort went public in the form of the Business Roundtable, a group of top American executives assuming direct responsibility for aggressively challenging what they perceived to be the antibusiness climate that was sweeping the country.[45]

NOTES

1. For a general overview see Frederick G. Dutton, *Changing Sources of Power: American Politics in the 1970s* (New York: McGraw-Hill Co., 1971); William L. O'Neill, *Coming Apart: An Informal History of America in the 1960s* (Chicago: Quadrangle Books, 1974); and Peter N. Carroll, *It Seemed Like Nothing Happened: The Tragedy and Promise of America in the 1970s* (New York: Holt, Rinehart and Winston, 1982).

2. Franz Schurmann, *The Foreign Politics of Richard Nixon: The Grand Design* (Berkeley: University of California Press, 1987).

3. Nixon had stated during the presidential campaign of 1968 that he would reduce or eliminate the controls as soon as possible.

4. *Congressional Quarterly Almanac, 1969*, pp. 809–810 (henceforth cited as *CQA*).

5. Ibid.

6. Ibid., p. 810.

7. Ibid., pp. 53A–55A, quote on pp. 53A–54A (emphasis added).

8. Ibid., pp. 87, 88.

9. Ibid., pp. 434–447.

The foreign aid "appropriation" bill was rejected by the Senate on December 20, 1969, by a vote to table the House-Senate conference report. Ibid., pp. 448–453.

10. Ibid., *1970*, pp. 130–132.

11. Nixon's trade policy message was sent to Congress on Nov. 18, 1969. It is conveniently found in ibid., *1969*, pp. 95A–97A.

This message's reference to the "multinational corporation" is, to the best of my knowledge, the first time the expression was used in an official public statement of a president.

12. The message is most conveniently reprinted in ibid., *1970*, pp. 54A–83A. The portion of the message on international economic policy is on pp. 71A–73A, quote on p. 72A.

13. Ibid. This message, formally outlining the "Nixon Doctrine," was also referred to as a "State of the World" message.

14. Ibid., pp. 989–991.

The report of the "Task Force" headed by Rudolph A. Peterson, former president of the Bank of America, should not be confused with the Peter G. Peterson study that was released in December, 1971, which is discussed below.

15. Ibid., pp. 992–997.

16. See chapter 4.

17. For background see Duane Kujawa, ed., *American Labor and the Multinational Corporation* (New York: Praeger Publishers, 1973) and David Brody, "The Expansion of the American Labor Movement: Institutional Sources of Stimulus and Restraint" in *Institutions in Modern America: Innovation in Structure and Process*, ed. by Stephen E. Ambrose (Baltimore: The Johns Hopkins University Press, 1967), pp. 11–36.

18. U.S. Congress, Joint Economic Committee, Subcommittee on Foreign Economic Policy, Hearings before . . . , *A Foreign Economic Policy for the 1970s, Part 2—Trade Policy Toward Developed Countries* (Washington: G.P.O., 1970), pp. 161–455.

19. Ibid., p. 367.

20. Ibid., pp. 372–377, quote on p. 377.

21. Ibid., p. 381.

22. U.S. Congress, Joint Economic Committee, Subcommittee on Foreign Economic Policy, Hearings before . . . , *A Foreign Economic Policy for the 1970s, Part 4—The Multinational Corporation and International Investment* (Washington: G.P.O., 1970), pp. 745–958.

These were the first formal hearings on the multinational corporation. The sixteen witnesses, while generally sympathetic to the activities of multinational corporations, lacked a common focus and many of the witnesses were more concerned about the impact of the multinational corporation on the world economy than its position vis-à-vis the U.S. government.

23. *CQA, 1970,* 105A–110A.

24. *Facts on File, 1971,* p. 119 and *CQA, 1971,* pp. 425–426. Quote in *Facts on File.*

25. U.S. Congress, Senate, Committee on Finance, Subcommittee on International Trade, Hearings before . . . , *Foreign Trade, World Trade and Investment Issues, Part 1* (Washington: G.P.O., 1971), pp. 1–487.

26. Ibid., *Part 2, Appendixes,* pp. 887–906.

27. Ibid., *Part 1* (hearings), pp. 1–487.

28. Ibid., pp. 168–173, quote on p. 168.

29. Ibid., pp. 180–185 (emphasis added).

30. Freeman's testimony may be found ibid., pp. 462–473; Ball's, ibid., pp. 336–338. See also ibid., pp. 356–361 for a prior address by Ball that had been inserted into the record as a fuller explanation of his views.

31. U.S. President, Report of Commission on International Trade and Investment Policy, *International Economic Policy in an Interdependent World, Report of . . . ,* I; *Papers of . . . ,* II and III (Washington: G.P.O., 1971).

32. Ibid., *Report of . . . ,* I, pp. 1–17, quotes from pp. 8, 14, 15 respectively.

33. Ibid., pp. 169–179, 182–184.

34. Ibid., pp. 32–34, quote on p. 34.

35. Ibid., pp. 277–279.

The Council on International Economic Policy (CIEP) should not be confused with the Council on Foreign Economic Policy (CFEP) established by Eisenhower in 1954 (see chapter 3).

36. Nixon's announced change in U.S. monetary policy, in effect a departure from at least a portion of the Bretton Woods agreements of 1945, is given its contextual significance in W. M. Scammell, *The International Economy Since 1945,* 2nd. ed. (New York: St. Martin's Press, 1983), p. 182. The domestic side of his new economic policy is briefly explained in Gilbert C. Fite and Jim E. Reese, *An Economic History of the United States,* 3rd ed. (Boston: Houghton Mifflin Co., 1973), pp. 577–578. The fullest factual account of the adjustments in Nixon's economic policy can be found in Lester A. Sobel, ed., *Inflation and the Nixon Administration* (New York: Facts on File, 1974–75) I [1969–71], II [1972–74]. See also U.S. President, *Economic Report of the President . . . , 1972* (Washington: G.P.O., 1972), pp. 3, 142–153.

37. C. Fred Bergsten, Thomas Horst, and Theodore H. Moran, *American Multinationals and American Interests* (Washington: The Brookings Institution, 1978), pp. 111–112, and Charles Culhane, "Labor [and] Industry Gear [Up] for Major Battle Over Bill to Curb Imports, Multinational," *National Journal* (January 15, 1972), pp. 108–119.

38. U.S. President, *The United States in a Changing World Economy*: I, *A Foreign Economic Perspective* by Peter G. Peterson, II, *Background Material* (Washington: G.P.O., 1972).

This study should not be confused with the report of a "Task Force" headed by Rudolph A. Peterson. See note 14.

39. Ibid., *Background . . .* , II, 48.

40. *Facts on File, 1972*, p. 229.

41. *CQA, 1972*, pp. 207–218 passim.

42. U.S. Congress, Senate, Committee on Foreign Relations, Subcommittee on Multinational Corporations, *Multinational Corporations and United States Foreign Policy*, Part 2 (Washington: G.P.O., 1973), speech by Senator Frank Church, reprinted in Appendix I, pp. 517–521.

43. Ibid., Part 1, pp. 1–3.

44. U.S. Congress, Senate, Finance Committee, Subcommittee on International Trade, Papers solicited by . . . , *Multinational Corporations, A Compendium of Papers* . . . (Washington: G.P.O., 1973). The "compendium" is 968 pages long.

45. Memo of Elliot Haynes of Business International, February 2, 1973 [typescript, unnumbered]. Baker Library, Harvard Business School, Boston, MA.

See also Leonard and Mark Silk, *The American Establishment* (New York: Avon Books, 1981), pp. 253–255.

6 CONGRESS AND THE SHIFT TO A MORE CRITICAL ATTITUDE: 1973–1974

In the early '70s America seemed to be at war with itself:

> The causes of the pervasive mood of alienation are variously identified as the Vietnam war, pollution, crowding, social inequalities, and all the disconcerting aspects of modern life. Whatever the causes, the extent of that alienation has been higher in recent years than at any time since World War II.
>
> The multinational enterprise cannot escape the consequences of the pervasive unease in the industrialized world. It is visible, powerful, and influential. It is thought of mainly as a product of American culture. So it stands on the barricades with the other questioned symbols of contemporary industrial society.[1]

And the barricades of multinational corporations were breached almost before those concerned knew what was happening. 1973 became a watershed year for the multinational corporation as well as for so many other symbols of American power.[2]

Serious international monetary problems captured the attention of the government as the Vietnam war issue gradually drifted off the front pages of our newspapers and lost its prominent place on the evening network news. The Nixon administration responded to this crisis on February 12, 1973, by announcing a 10 percent devaluation of the U.S. dollar against nearly all the world's currencies. It was hoped that this action would halt the speculative selling of dollars for West German marks and Japanese yen by bankers and large corporations anticipating a revaluation of these currencies against the dollar. It was also intended to address, from a different perspective, the twin domestic problems of inflation and growing unemployment.[3]

What went virtually unnoticed in this preoccupation with a worsening economic climate was a 930 page report on the multinational corporation that many subsequently considered a benchmark study. Unfortunately, the study was released on February 12, 1973, the same day the dollar devaluation was announced. Authored by the U.S. Tariff Commission for the Senate Finance Committee's Subcommittee on International Trade, the massive report carried the unwieldy title *Implications of Multinational Firms for World Trade and Investment and for U.S. Trade and Labor.* Comprehensive in scope, it covered everything from "antitrust" to "world patterns of investment."

As might be expected, the study was generally favorable to the policies and priorities of multinational corporations based in the United States, saying that they "did not dominate" world trade; they exerted "significant influence" on the rates and patterns of fixed capital formation in many host countries; they played a larger role as exporters than as importers in terms of their impact on U.S. trade; and they appeared to have a positive rather than a negative effect on employment in America—but that final judgement on this issue would have to be made on an industry-by-industry basis. On the question of influencing the balance of payments profile, the study concluded that the multinational corporation played "no role" in America's poor performance. In terms of its role in the international money market, the study insisted that while the multinational corporation "created" the international money market, this form of economic activity had subsequently become institutionalized, thereby removing the multinational corporation from any "destructive" or "predatory" influence, even if it was so inclined to act under these motives.[4]

If it was a dispassionate study, it was not an unusable one, and Senator Abraham Ribicoff, the chairman of the Subcommittee on International Trade, used it to showcase his hearings on the multinational corporation. Thus, while Senator Frank Church's Subcommittee on Multinational Corporations was busily collecting information on the activities of ITT's representatives in Washington and in Chile, Ribicoff's subcommittee opened their own hearings on the multinational corporation on February 26, 1973.

He wasted no time in placing his subcommittee's hearings into the broadest possible context:

Members of the committee, the latest international monetary crisis leading to the second devaluation of the dollar in less than two years is another dramatic reminder that the international trading community has not put its house in order.

This nation's economic standing in the world is at a low point. We have one of the highest rates of unemployment of all the industrialized nations. We have gone from a $7 billion trade surplus in 1964 to a $7 billion trade deficit last year. . . .

Part of the problem is that we are today dealing with a new phenomena that requires new understanding before solutions can be offered. Increasingly questions are being asked about the role American multinational corporations have been playing in currency movements and the export of American jobs and technology as well as the implications of their operations on national interests. . . .

During the past few years they have become the focus of controversy in our own country and have increasingly come under attack. In covering aspects of the operation of the multinationals, I realize we will be getting into discussions of basic foreign economic policies. I welcome this. All of us concerned with these problems welcome the fullest and frankest treatment of these issues.[5]

Ribicoff virtually dominated every phase of the hearings, regularly interrupting witnesses and even fellow senators with negative or inquisitive questions. He created the impression that this was the first time anyone had ever seriously questioned the impact of the multinational corporation on the domestic or international economy.

Because the hearings also dealt with the reintroduced Burke-Hartke bill, organized labor's initial effort to restrict the multinational corporation, several union leaders promptly seized the opportunity to vigorously itemize their growing list of complaints against the multinational corporation.[6] Leonard Woodcock, the president of the United Auto Workers, while not appearing as a witness, submitted a carefully prepared statement calling for both national and international regulatory legislation to address the "new problem" created by the "rise of the MNCs [multinational corporations]."[7] In calling for action on the Burke-Hartke bill, however, labor's most aggressive witnesses were Andrew Biemiller, director of legislation for the AFL-CIO, and Nathaniel Goldfinger, the union's director of research. Their testimony and impressive supporting documentation left little doubt that by 1973 labor had became critical of virtually all aspects of corporate multinationalization.[8] Testimony in support of the multinational corporation came from two administration witnesses, Peter Flangan, the executive director of the President's Council on Economic Policy, and Frederick Dent, the Secretary of Commerce. In addition, two respected representatives of corporate America also testified. The first was Thomas Murphy, the vice-chairman of General Motors, the other Gilbert Jones, the chairman of IBM World Trade Corporation.[9]

But much of this formal testimony was overshadowed by the unscheduled appearance of Russell Long, the chairman of the Senate Finance Committee, to which this subcommittee ultimately would report, and Senator Vance Hartke, also a member of the Finance Committee. Long, who questioned Biemiller before he had had an opportunity to read his opening statement, suggested to labor's principal spokesman at these hearings that the unions had reversed themselves in supporting foreign aid and liberal trade policies because these policies ultimately led to the exporting of jobs to the detriment of the American worker. Biemiller acknowledged that up until 1963 labor had supported liberal—but not free—trade policies. Since then, they had studied the issue and, "about four years ago," the entire labor movement did a "real complete turnabout."[10]

Long's response to this acknowledgment of labor's critical attitude focused on trade imbalance and a general observation that labor was being hurt by this imbalance without any specific reference to multinational corporations. He either missed, or deliberately ignored, Biemiller's point that labor had adopted a different attitude toward U.S. trade policy because the growth of multinational corporations had altered the circumstances that, in the past, allowed them to support a moderately liberal trade policy.[11]

Hartke's presence at these hearings was more reflective of his prolabor point of view than it was useful to the subcommittee. He seized the occasion to get his own views on the record, ignoring the disclaimers and qualifying statements of those who were supportive of multinational corporations, making it clear he had little sympathy for, or appreciation of, the arguments of those who supported the multinationalization of corporate America. From his perspective, organized labor's criticism of the multinational corporation was thoroughly justified.[12]

In spite of the hearings of Ribicoff's subcommittee, the findings of the U.S. Tariff Commission's benchmark study failed to have an impact on the country's understanding of the role of the multinational corporation in America. This study, as well as all previous studies, was quickly overshadowed by the spectacular testimony that came out of the much publicized hearings of the Subcommittee on Multinational Corporations. When these hearings opened on March 20, 1973, some two weeks after Ribicoff's subcommittee had ended its series of hearings, it triggered a massive inquiry into the men, means, and methods associated with the multinationalization of corporate America. The stage was set for an exhaustive investigation at the very moment the Nixon administration was trying—albeit not very successfully—to formulate a meaningful international economic policy for the '70s.

Between March 20 and April 2 the Senate Subcommittee on Multinational Corporations paraded before the news media a string of witnesses that, while differing with one another on detail, disclosed that ITT had twice offered $1 million to the U.S. government to support any plan to help block the election of Marxist candidate Salvador Allende Gossens as president of Chile. At the time, ITT's investment in Chile amounted to an estimated $160 million that ITT expected to lose if Allende came to power and implemented his campaign promise to expropriate the assets of foreign multinational companies in the country. The ITT offer was communicated to the Nixon administration by John A. McCone, a member of ITT's board of directors and a former head and current consultant of the CIA. The offer was made to Henry Kissinger, Nixon's principal advisor on foreign policy matters at that time, and to Richard Helms, the current head of the CIA.[13]

In his testimony before Church's subcommittee, McCone was perfectly candid about why he had contacted Helms. He wished:

. . . to reflect to him and, through him, to the policy makers of the Government the views of the foreign people in ITT [i.e., those responsible for the foreign operations of the company] concerning the probable outcome of the 1970 elections. . . .

He continued:

I felt that our Government should be alerted to the consequences of the election, not only because of its effects on the business interests, but also because of the effects on the taxpayer. Because there were, as you know, several hundred million dollars of OPIC guarantees, of which approximately $100 million were ITT's. . . .

Church interrupted:

Senator Church: Mr. McCone, do you mean that the fact that OPIC, in part a federally financed insurance agency, had insured the ITT properties against expropriation, created an identity of interests between ITT and the U.S. Government, or at least created a close common interest?

Mr. McCone: No; I don't think it necessarily created an identity of interest. The point I was making was that if the policies of Mr. Allende were carried out, both parties would suffer.[14]

In one day, March 21, 1973, the matter-of-fact testimony of one of this country's most knowledgeable corporate lawyers and a former head of the CIA put the multinational corporation into a totally new perspective. McCone was candidly admitting that ITT was trying to influence American foreign policy so that the U.S. government would cooperate with them to manipulate an election in a foreign country. Apparently, ITT considered these initiatives as appropriate behavior, given the economic vulnerability of a taxpayer-financed agency of the Federal government (i.e., OPIC) and the fact that Allende was perceived to be a Marxist. The web of interdependence that unfolded so casually in this one day of testimony was so breathtaking that few at the time appreciated its implications.

And how, Church asked, was the $1 million to be used? McCone said for low-cost housing, agricultural needs, and technical assistance. Subsequently, the CIA's designated contact with ITT, William Broe, testified that it was his understanding that the money was to be used by the CIA to create economic chaos to block Allende's election. Infuriated by the contradictions, Church declared that someone was lying and that the testimony was getting "curiouser and curiouser" [sic].[15]

The immediate result was a recommendation by the Subcommittee on Multinational Corporations that a law be passed making it a criminal offense for U.S. citizens or corporations to offer money to the Federal government to help finance American intervention into a foreign country to alter the outcome of an election in that country. The subcommittee also agreed to make OPIC the focus of the next phase of its investigation. The law recommended by Church's subcommittee passed the Senate but was never voted on by the House.[16] The decision to focus on OPIC dramatically expanded the scope of the subcommittee's investigation. Multinational corporations could readily disassociate themselves from the specifics of ITT's Chilean adventures, but an investigation into OPIC's practices vis-à-vis private foreign investments seemed to put all multinational corporations that had used OPIC on the defensive.

But before the subcommittee's investigation of OPIC got underway, the White House involvement in the June, 1972, break-in of the Democratic national headquarters in the Watergate complex in Washington redefined the political climate in the nation's capital. E. Howard Hunt, J. Gordon Liddy, and James Dean suddenly became more newsworthy than John A. McCone and William Broe, as one opinion poll after another chronicled the country's growing conviction that Nixon was lying about his staff's involvement in the Watergate break-in and, ultimately, his own personal involvement in this affair. Domestic inflation and constant reversals by the Nixon administration on wage and price controls all suggested that the administration had lost its sense of direction and was flailing away at its multiple problems and mounting embarrassments.

Yet, during the time that Church's subcommittee was collecting data on ITT, a small group of specialists working inside the ornate Old State Department building were putting into final form what would become a historic document, the first *International Economic Report of the President to Congress*. Annual economic reports has been produced since 1946, but 1973 was the first year that an "international" economic report had been prepared by the executive branch of government.

In the past, international economic policy had always been an afterthought, the proverbial last—or next to last—chapter in every president's annual or semiannual economic report to Congress. But in 1973 a specialized cabinet-level group, the Council on International Economic Policy (CIEP), established in 1971 by presidential memorandum and given formal legal status by the International Economic Policy Act of 1972, produced an exhaustive analysis of America's international economic position in the global economy. The idea of a specialized cabinet-level group to advise the President on international economic policy was not Nixon's, but when it was recommended to him by the President's Advisory Council on Executive Organization, he promptly implemented their recommendation. He thus became the first president to recognize that this was one area of policy-making that had become so complex and so sensitive that separate policy-review machinery was necessary to coordinate the perspectives of the several departments and agencies within the executive branch that had responsibilities in the field of international economic policy.[17]

Unfortunately, this 1973 *International Economic Report* was never given the reading it deserved by anyone, including, probably, the beleaguered President himself. Yet it advanced an analysis of the global economy that put the role of multinational corporations into perspective, leaving little doubt as to their importance. However, the report also insisted that certain fundamental changes in international economic policy and in our trading system must be addressed first.[18]

As a result, multinational corporations were not discussed extensively until Chapter 5 in the seven chapter report. Here they were described as the "main instrument" for integrating "capital, technology, and management" and "the continually diminishing cost of transporting materials," allowing for "more and more beneficial combinations of elements of production." Despite the "benefits," there were critics, and there were problems:

> Where the evidence suggests some new harm from the investment activities of multi-national corporations, those activities must be promptly addressed. Where net gain is found, multinational corporate activities should be encouraged. The art of sensible policy development will be to maintain the benefits of international investment while alleviating harmful side effects.[19]

But for many in Congress, the die was cast; multinational corporations were being viewed as the cause of many of our problems. Even if the President's reputation had been beyond reproach, the findings of the Council on International Economic Policy were too judicious to influence the course of events.

Like no event since World War II, the ITT investigation had given the multinational corporation greater visibility, promoting an interest in several recently released studies presuming to examine all the problems associated with the corporate multinationalization process. These studies, all looking back on the previous decade, reviewed the role of the multinational corporation with respect to domestic employment, technology transfer, balance of payments, and the multinational's response to investment controls. Carefully structured case studies addressed the "motivation" of U.S. multinational enterprises and the "apparent causes" of why American companies elected to engage in foreign direct investments. The focus was on the past, on the when's, where's, and why's corporate America went multinational.[20] But this was 1973, after the ITT investigation had caused many in government to question the implications of the multinationalization process. The focus had suddenly shifted, from an historical analysis of causes, to the frequently significant geopolitical and ethical consequences of corporate multinationalization.

Some measure of the changing attitude toward the consequences of the multinationalization process can be found in the activities of an obscure subcommittee of the House Committee on Foreign Affairs, i.e., the Subcommittee on Africa. In May of 1971, this subcommittee had opened hearings on U.S. business involvement in southern Africa. The subcommittee heard from the Polaroid Revolutionary Workers Movement, the associate administrators of the "tracking" and "data acquisition" operations of NASA, church groups, Gulf Oil, the Export-Import Bank, and representatives of the State and Commerce Departments at the deputy-assistant secretary level. Each witness testified as to the employment practices of his organization in the Republic of South Africa. The word "multinational" was seldom used, never pejoratively. The issue was apartheid and the extent to which U.S. business practices constituted a *de facto* or *de jure* endorsement of this policy. The hearings attracted little attention.[21] A second series of hearings were held between September 27 and December 7, 1971, with essentially the same focus.[22]

The subcommittee did not hold any further hearings on "U.S. business involvement in Southern Africa [sic]" until March of 1973, more than fifteen months later. When it did resume hearings on this topic, its focus had been expanded to include "U.S. government *policy* with respect to U.S. business involvement in this area" and "U.S. government *support, encouragement, facilitation* and *protection* of such businesses."[23] In effect, the Subcommittee on Africa had joined the ranks of those congressional committees investigating the practices of the multinational corporations and the extent to which the U.S. government was a party to these practices.

Over a two-year period this subcommittee's investigation had gradually shifted from an inquiry into U.S. businesses' and U.S. government agencies' "involvement" with apartheid to an inquiry into U.S. government support and protection of businesses that, by their conduct, condoned apartheid. When the third phase of these hearings resumed in March of 1973, the appropriate response to apartheid had also changed. Previously, American businesses in South Africa were expected to do nothing that "supported" apartheid, now American businesses were expected to "get out of South Africa." "Disengagement" was the only acceptable course of action, and anyone advocating a more compromising policy was automatically on the defensive, i.e., most American multinational corporations with facilities in South Africa, the Departments of State and Commerce, NASA, the Atomic Energy Commission, and OPIC.[24]

In May, 1973, as this Subcommittee on Africa was completing its work, a second House subcommittee was opening "oversight hearings" on the "policy" and "operations" of OPIC. This second subcommittee, the Subcommittee on Foreign Economic Policy, serving as the investigative arm of the House Foreign Affairs Committee, was charged with the responsibility of making recommendations as to the future of OPIC, due to expire on June 30, 1974. The subcommittee's chairman, John C. Culver of Iowa, said the investigation was necessary "... because of the growing concern about the role of the U.S. multinational corporation and heightened economic nationalism in the developing world."[25] The subcommittee held nine days of essentially technical hearings through May and June, and issued its report in October. While critical of OPIC, it accepted the administration's recommendation that the agency be allowed to continue for two years beyond its scheduled expiration date. It insisted, however, that certain safeguards be written into the new bill to prevent multinational corporations from using the agency to build a partnership with the Federal government if they faced difficulties with a foreign government. An eventual phase-out of OPIC was an implicit part of their report.[26]

While this subcommittee report was being prepared, the more prominent Subcommittee on Multinational Corporations was resuming its hearings, using its ITT revelations as a justification for undertaking its own review of OPIC's investment guarantee program and management policy. Whereas the House's Subcommittee on Foreign Economic Policy had focused on the operations of OPIC, the Subcommittee on Multinational Corporations focused on the policies of the multinational corporations and the extent to which OPIC supported these policies rather than the agency's basic legislative mandate to promote foreign investment in underdeveloped countries. The questioning was not hostile, but the premise of at least the Democratic members of the subcommittee was that OPIC seemed to be more concerned about the multinational corporation than it was about the underdeveloped countries in which these corporations operated. When the former U.S. ambassador to Jamaica, Vincent deRoulet, testified that he had "implied" to one of the island's candidates for prime minister that if the expropriation of the island's American-owned bauxite/alumina industry was made an election issue, the United States might have to intervene in the election because of the immense OPIC insurance coverage that the agency had written for that industry, the subcommittee promptly concluded that it had uncovered another ITT-type case.[27] It was testimony like this that prompted the subcommittee to recommend that Congress phase out, or transfer to the private sector, the insurance program of OPIC and terminate, or shift to other agencies, the direct financing functions of the agency.[28] It was argued that the linkage was so obvious and inevitable that only a complete severance of the relationship would ensure a permanent solution.

The evidence gathered by these three congressional subcommittees (i.e., the Subcommittee on Africa, the Subcommittee on Foreign Economic Policy, and the Subcommittee on Multinational Corporations) suggested that not only did OPIC serve the multinational corporation but, ironically, from an administrative point of view, it really had no other choice. The language of the law establishing the agency required that OPIC only finance projects deemed to be low risk, and that the agency write only actuarially-defensible insurance coverage to protect its own solvency. Thus the language of the law establishing the agency virtually ruled out most developmental-type projects, which had been the avowed purpose of OPIC when it was established in 1969 as an alternative to the Agency for International Development.[29]

This series of Congressional hearings revealed a further dimension to the OPIC story. Apparently most multinational corporations never approached OPIC for a loan or insurance coverage unless they had a valid reason for making the foreign investment in the first instance. The foreign investment decisions of multinational corporations were usually calculated corporate assessments of projected profits from these investments. Once that investment decision had been made, the only further decision was whether the company should approach OPIC for a loan to help finance the project. In areas judged to be politically unstable, there was also the question of whether it was necessary and financially feasible to carry OPIC insurance, and whether that insurance should be written to include outright expropriation, protection against currency nonconvertibility in case of a forced buy-out, and war risks—or all three.

Apparently many multinational corporations were saying, in effect, "thanks, but no thanks." All other things being equal, the prudent corporate response to political instability was to avoid the country in question—not buy some form of OPIC insurance. Those corporations that elected to use OPIC's loan or insurance services clearly wanted to initiate a partnership with the U.S. government to protect an investment that they considered essential to their survival. This was most evident in the extractive industries where access to raw materials was essential to their survival even if the country or region was politically unstable. OPIC critics insisted that in such a situation, the corporation might well have been more interested in State Department support in case of a problem, than in the actual OPIC insurance to protect its interests.[30]

Both the House Foreign Affairs Committee and the Senate Foreign Relations Committee, faced with distasteful examples of government-corporate linkage and with evidence of a fundamental irreconcilability between developmental assistance and OPIC solvency, reluctantly recommended that the agency be continued.[31] For the immediate future its insurance functions were to be shared with private insurance companies and its financing operations hedged by innovative investment devices such as joint ventures with host-country firms or banks, arrangements that presumably would lessen the likelihood of expropriation in politically unstable areas of the world. The language of the bill as it emerged from Congress further compromised the OPIC's developmental mandate and seemed to presuppose its eventual demise.[32] Multinational corporations, never enthusiastic about OPIC, had already started to look elsewhere for financing.

It must also be recognized that these OPIC hearings only received marginal attention in the executive suites of the most prominent multinational corporations. What was happening in the crowded chamber of another Senate conference room was for more important to them than the future of OPIC.

The hearings of a Select Senate Committee on Watergate under the chairmanship of the venerable Senator Sam Irvin of North Carolina brought virtually the whole inner circle of the Nixon White House into disrepute. Nixon had never been corporate America's favorite president and the systematic shakedown in 1972 of many of the nation's largest corporations by the Committee to Re-elect the President did nothing to enhance his image. Many considered him too self-serving to qualify as a friend of business, or any other interest group for that matter. But the Watergate hearings made corporate executives uncomfortable. A George Steinbrenner might openly complain about an "old-fashioned Goddamn shakedown" by Nixon's associates, and candidly admit his shipbuilding firm had been threatened with investigations by the Justice Department, the IRS, and the Department of Commerce; yet most corporate executives preferred to avoid publicizing such embarrassing threats. They might have enjoyed seeing Nixon under attack, but they had no desire to see their ties with either political party come under close public scrutiny.[33]

This was certainly a less than favorable political climate for what followed, a scenario which damaged the credibility of the multinational corporation. On October 8, 1973, representatives of the major foreign and American oil companies, i.e., the "Seven Sisters," met with the oil ministers of the Arab states that were members of the Organization of Petroleum Exporting Countries (OPEC). At the time, OPEC was considered little more than a loosely formed cartel of oil producing nations. The context for this meeting in Vienna was a decision by OPEC to exploit the current world oil shortage to secure an increase in the price of crude oil.

But there was more. For months the so-called pro-American block of Arab states in OPEC, led by Saudi Arabia, had been warning the American oil companies that they must urge their government to abandon its open support for Israel or see America's oil supplies constricted. The warning was duly transmitted by the American oil companies, with the Nixon administration being told quite bluntly that its assistance to Israel was undermining the multinational oil companies' rapidly eroding influence in the Arab world. The warning apparently fell on deaf ears. Most students of Middle East affairs, including specialists in the State Department, misjudged the power of OPEC, believing that the Arab oil producing countries in the Middle East so distrusted one another that they could never agree on, much less implement, a common policy. Congress, accepting the assessment of the government's specialists, steadfastly endorsed the traditional pro-Israeli policy of the United States.

With unfathomable irony, the representatives of the multinational oil companies found themselves meeting OPEC's oil ministers in Vienna on October 8th, only two days after the outbreak of the Yom Kippur War. The news media focused not on this seemingly routine meeting in Vienna, but on the war, stressing the prowess of the Israeli army and the apparent ineptness of their Egyptian opponents. While the executives of the multinational oil companies talked about the need to increase supplies and the technical financial arrangements they expected from the Arab states to ensure an adequate margin of profit, the oil ministers passed around newspaper clippings and photographs showing American military supplies going to Israel and pointedly took note of existing oil shortages in the West and America's obsessively pro-Israeli foreign policy. By October 11th, the meeting had collapsed, a total failure. Furthermore, the OPEC oil ministers announced that they intended to meet again among themselves in Kuwait on the 17th to discuss oil as a weapon of war. Suddenly, the issues of price and supply were transformed into the threat of an oil embargo.

On the 17th, the OPEC ministers agreed to raise prices on their crude oil, then on the 18th, the Arab members of OPEC agreed to an immediate 5 percent cutback on oil production, to be adjusted downward by 5 percent during each succeeding month until Israeli troops withdrew from all Arab territories that had been occupied since "the June 1967 War." In a matter of days, Saudi Arabia, the largest supplier, plus Bahrain, Kuwait, Qatar, and Dubai outdid the other Arab states by imposing a complete embargo on any country that had a record of consistently supporting Israel.[34]

The same day the Vienna meeting collapsed, October 11th, the Senate Foreign Relations Committee's Subcommittee on Multinational Corporations opened hearings on "Multinational Petroleum Companies and U.S. Foreign Policy." This third phase of the subcommittee's hearings investigated, in executive session, the way the oil companies responded to a 1970–1971 demand by Colonel Quadaffi of Libya for a significant increase in the price of Libyan oil. Quadaffi, as distrusted by the Gulf members of OPEC as by the oil companies operating in Libya, had threatened to nationalize the holdings of the so-called "independents" if they did not accept the price increases he demanded. It was a serious threat, for the "independents" were the smaller oil companies that relied almost exclusively on Libyan oil for their supply.

The members of the subcommittee listened with fascination as the representatives of the oil industry explained how, in 1970, they had devised a strategy to thwart Quadaffi. They had formed a united front against him by establishing something known as the "London Policy Group" to deprive the Libyan leader of the option of "picking them off" one by one. The executives noted that, at the time, they were also concerned that the formation of this "Group" might be viewed by the Antitrust Division of the Justice Department as a violation of America's antitrust laws. To avoid possible prosecution under the Sherman or Clayton Antitrust acts, they asked the State Department to request a "business review letter" from the Antitrust Division of the Justice Department that would exempt them from prosecution because of this prearranged common negotiating mechanism. The Antitrust Division, while receptive to the request of the

State Department, wrote a "business review letter" that carefully limited the area of prosecution-exempt negotiations.[35]

In the broader perspective, this was merely another example of the government helping multinational oil companies; accepting the fact that, like most extractive industries, they needed considerable latitude and assistance when it came to maintaining their source of supply. But the testimony emerging from these hearings on Libya documented what many suspected—the multinational oil companies were working very closely with the State Department and were, in fact, fashioning the parameters of our relations with Libya. What few observers in Washington realized was that the collapse of the talks between the oil companies and the members of OPEC on October 11th had far more ominous implications for the future than anything revealed by these Libyan hearings.

The winter of 1973–1974 destroyed the credibility of virtually all multinational oil companies dependent on Middle East oil. Just as they were being charged with virtually fashioning American foreign policy toward the oil producing states of the Middle East, getting the State Department to do their bidding because of their "special needs" as an extractive industry, the tables were turned and they were suddenly perceived as pawns of these oil producing nations. Throughout the winter the companies were engaged in damage control on several fronts. Their consumers, literally all of Western Europe, Japan, the United States, and the developing nations in the Third World, were demanding oil, forcing the companies to juggle their limited supplies. At the same time, the companies dared not antagonize the oil producing Arab states so necessary to their survival as multinational enterprises when and if the embargo ended.

But while the major oil companies dramatically moved their supertankers among the world's oceans as if playing a global chess game, the price of oil climbed to staggering heights. The iron laws of supply and demand gave the oil companies profits so enormous that even they ultimately admitted that they had difficulty grasping the full implications of their sudden wealth, and they found themselves "playing God" with what suddenly appeared to be the world's most essential natural resource. The executives of these companies would subsequently testify about how uncomfortable they were as arbiters of the economies of much of the industrialized world. Yet it was also obvious that they did not know how to curb their instinct for maximum profits. This was particularly true when they realized that they might suddenly lose the principal source of their wealth if the Arab oil producing states in OPEC decided to take control of the whole extraction, refining, and distribution process and deal directly with the consuming nations. The contradictions were everywhere, and everyone had to live with them.[36]

The American consumer, waiting in long lines to purchase gas at prices that doubled in a matter of months, blamed not the Arab oil producing states, but the oil companies whose familiar signs dotted the nation's landscape. In the process, the average consumer learned these companies were not just American oil companies—they were multinational enterprises. They were businesses that were so large that they had virtually all the attributes of a national state. And these oil companies were in fact only one breed of multinational corporation; the corporate world was full of them.

When the Senate Watergate Committee, whose televised hearings everyone was watching, uncovered the fact that Gulf and Ashland oils had broken the law by making secret contributions to help finance Nixon's reelection campaign in 1972, everyone hung on the sordid details. The vast television audience learned that Gulf had an office in Washington, presided over by someone who was a "vice president for government relations," and that this corporate officer, as a matter of policy, had systematically laundered the company's $100,000 contribution to Nixon's election campaign through a Gulf subsidiary in the Bahamas in order to get around Federal election laws.[37]

The Watergate hearings, the embargo, the escalating cost of gas and heating oil, and the enormous profits being amassed by the multinational oil companies breathed new life into the Senate Foreign Relations Committee's Subcommittee on Multinational Corporations. The subcommittee chose to resume its hearings on the theme "Multinational Petroleum Companies and U.S. Foreign Policy," which had been the focus for their Libyan investigation in October, 1973. This time they were, in the words of the chairman Frank Church, "uncovering a trail [of arrangements] ... that led the United States into a dependency on the Arab sheikdoms for ... much of its oil." "Why," he asked rhetorically and substantively, "did our government support and encourage the movement of the huge American-owned oil companies into the Middle East in the first place?"[38] The stage was set for an exhaustive inquiry into how America's multinational oil companies had operated in the Middle East since roughly the end of World War II. But more importantly, the subcommittee's investigation also raised questions as to what degree the American government had abdicated its responsibility to formulate a viable foreign policy with the Arab states in the Middle East in order to salvage or insulate its pro-Israeli policy. Was it really letting businessmen fashion the linkage between the Arab oil producing countries of the Middle East and the oil consuming nations of the West?

The evidence uncovered by the subcommittee seemed to suggest that the abdication was virtually total. In the decade following the end of World War II, the U.S. government encouraged and assisted the American oil companies to become the principal suppliers of oil for the West. Allowing the oil companies to negotiate for adequate supplies for the United States and for the West while providing the producing countries with generous profits in return was, in effect, a form of indirect or "backdoor" foreign aid to Arab states. Tax concessions and such things as "business review letters" were merely a part of the process. The oil companies had fashioned a pseudo-Middle East foreign policy *for* the United States, and no one in the Federal government seemed to be monitoring their activities.[39]

Ambassador David Newsome's testimony before the Subcommittee on Multinational Corporations said it all:

It has generally been the practice over the years and the one that has been sought by both [multinational oil] companies and the [U.S.] government that the basic relationship of the individual companies to a foreign government are the exclusive province virtually of those two. The U.S. government becomes involved only when there is some general problem.[40]

Testimony before the Subcommittee on Multinational Corporations revealed more than an abdication of responsibility. OPEC had been an administrative entity since September, 1960, yet neither the State Department, the CIA, nor, apparently, any other governmental agency had ever assessed its possible impact on the operational patterns of the international oil industry. And no one in the Federal government or in the multinational oil companies apparently had ever seriously considered developing a spare or alternate production capacity.

All that changed in October, 1973.

The public, disinterested in the technical testimony before the subcommittee, instinctively blamed the oil companies. But those who monitored the subcommittee's activities through August, 1974, recognized that it had exposed a story of government ineptitude that was far more serious than the numerous instances of "favoritism" manifested by the various tax concessions or hastily issued "business review letters." The United States, with the industrialized West and Japan as largely silent accomplices, seemingly had allowed several multinational oil companies—five American and two foreign—to be the principal architects of a global oil policy.[41]

Quite independent of the hearings of this subcommittee and what they revealed, the embargo was as serious an economic crisis for the nation as Watergate was a political crisis. And, however discredited, the Nixon administration had to address the issue. The response to what was being called the "October Revolution" was threefold. On November 7, 1973, the President announced that the Federal government would initiate "Project Independence" to free America of its dependence on foreign energy sources by 1980. Second, following the hastily called Washington Energy Conference in February, 1974, the Federal government established an emergency sharing system for the major oil consuming nations of the world. Third, the U.S. government announced it would attempt to bring down oil prices by working with Saudi Arabia (already publicly committed to lowering prices) and by "recycling" OPEC revenues (currently being deposited by the oil producing states in the major capital markets of the United States and Europe) back into the economies of the consuming nations. Aside from the emergency sharing system, the various government initiatives were generally recognized as inadequate by October of 1974.[42]

But the most inexplicable feature of this policy was that the administration's initiatives in no way reacted to the past or current activities of the multinational oil companies. When questioned by the Senate's Subcommittee on Multinational Corporations, officials of the Nixon, and later the Ford, administrations gave conflicting testimony as to the need for, or propriety of, a changed policy toward the oil companies. There were no references to punishment. There was some discussion of an oversight role, but without controls. And there was some consideration given to simply allowing market forces to prevail. But the remedies mentioned were largely speculative. In the end, the Nixon administration even resisted any legislative initiative to review the existing tax law on foreign source income.[43]

What the first year of hearings by the Subcommittee on Multinational Corporations most clearly revealed was an ingrained institutionalized weakness in the Federal government when it came to monitoring the activities of the multinational oil companies. No one, it seems, had ultimate responsibility for formulating policy with respect to foreign oil matters. This administration, like the ones that had preceded it, had virtually no policy toward the multinational oil companies and, apparently, no intention of formulating one.[44]

In February, 1974, in the midst of the oil crisis, the Council on International Economic Policy (CIEP) released the second congressionally mandated *International Economic Report of the President.* Replete with graphs, diagrams, and statistical tables, it categorized the embargo and the consequent energy crisis into one of seven "select current international economic issues."[45]

The CIEP divided its *International Economic Report* into two parts. In Part I, "Progress Toward Achieving the Nation's International Goals," the multinational corporation figured prominently in a discussion of monetary policy with the observation that:

it is ncither the desire nor the intention of the [U.S.] government to become involved in every investment dispute that arises; often the parties can better settle their differences directly, or failing that, reach settlement through judicial means, including international dispute settlement mechanisms.[46]

Part II considered the seven "select current international economic issues," and took up the energy crisis in the first chapter of this section of the report. It carried no reference to the multinational oil companies. The first explicit reference to multinational corporations in Part II of the report came in Chapter 3 and was merely a restatement of the U.S. traditional openness to foreign-based multinational enterprises investing *in* the United States. It was Chapter 5 before the American multinational corporation was considered at length. The context was "international technology transfer" and the extent to which the transfer of technology by multinationals had compromised our "economic preeminence" in effect, exporting jobs and creating, in turn, domestic unemployment. The CIEP concluded that the research to date had produced *no* conclusive evidence that supported or refuted any of these charges against multinational enterprises.[47]

If the November, 1973, response of the administration to the embargo and this *International Economic Report* released in February, 1974, were any index, the Nixon administration had not even begun to address the questions that had been raised by the Subcommittee on Multinational Corporations on the linkage between multinational oil companies and U.S. foreign policy.

Throughout the early months of 1974, the hearings that generated the most serious allegations were those initiated by this increasingly influential Subcommittee on Multinational Corporations. The subcommittee had turned its attention to investigating the charges of columnist Jack Anderson that the Arab-American Oil Company, ARAMCO, a multinational enterprise that consisted of four American oil companies and Saudi Arabia, had conspired to increase oil prices at the well-head. It was an arrangement that had been in place long before the formation of OPEC. The disjointed nature of the hearings made it difficult to establish or refute Anderson's allegations, derived, he insisted, from confidential sources. But what became clear was that the Federal government was, at best, inattentive to the solutions ARAMCO worked out for itself to ensure easy access to Saudi Arabian oil.

The evidence suggested that the generous tax credits and distinctive accounting practices associated with the various types of oil company payments to Saudi Arabia and possibly the other oil producing countries did not begin to address the issue, namely, the need for conventional diplomacy to ensure a proper relationship between each of the producing countries and the U.S. government. Even the antitrust aspects of this issue—for the testimony indicated ARAMCO most certainly violated the spirit if not the substance of the Sherman and Clayton antitrust laws—brought forth an admission from a Justice Department witness that nothing was done because of "policy divergencies" among the several government departments and agencies that decided if, how, when, and where our antitrust laws would be applied. The deeper the Senate's subcommittee probed, the more sordid the story became.[48]

In June and July of 1974 the subcommittee expanded its investigation even further, looking into the activities of multinational corporations operating in Communist bloc countries. It focused in particular on a proposed natural gas project in the Soviet Union. This aspect of the subcommittee's investigation opened up a whole new set of questions about the compromising features of corporate multinationalization. The investigation ranged from the most obvious, namely, would such a project generate an ITT-OPIC type linkage between the construction companies and OPIC, to more complex questions of technology transfer and a fundamental shift in policy with respect to existing restrictions on East-West trade. And then there were the broader concerns about assisting Russia in securing a vital natural resource that might in turn compromise our own national security. The hearings, and the thorough staff report issued five months later, brought a host of troubling questions into clearer focus. But once again, there were no remedies. At best, this most recent set of hearings of the Subcommittee on Multinational Corporations reminded the State and Commerce Departments of Congress' basic oversight role, and it also reinforced the notion that it was the responsibility of these two departments to see to it that the multinational corporation never be allowed to define U.S. policy or even so much as color our basic objectives when we were dealing with any of the Communist bloc nations.[49]

But these areas of congressional inquiry by Church's Subcommittee on Multinational Corporations could not begin to compete for attention with the televised hearings of the House Judiciary Committee charged with determining if there was sufficient evidence to impeach the President. All other issues paled in comparison to the issues raised by these hearings, and then by the unprecedented constitutional crisis created by the unexpected resignation of Nixon from the presidency on August 8.

The eyes of the world were on a helicopter lifting off from the Rose Garden of the White House. The place of the multinational corporation in defining America's international economic policy was suddenly less significant.

NOTES

1. Raymond Vernon, *Storm over the Multinationals: The Real Issues* (Cambridge: Harvard University Press, 1977), pp. 137–138.

2. William H. Chafe, *The Unfinished Journey: America Since World War II* (New York: Oxford University Press, 1986), p. 447.

3. *Congressional Quarterly Almanac, 1973*, pp. 225–233 (henceforth cited as CQA).

4. U.S. Congress, Senate, Finance Committee, Subcommittee on International Trade, *Implications of Multinational Firms for World Trade and Investment and for U.S. Trade and Labor,* by the U.S. Tariff Commission for the Senate Finance Committee, Subcommittee on . . . , (Washington: G.P.O., 1973), quotes drawn from "Summary of Findings of the Study," pp. 1–14. See also *Facts on File, 1973,* p. 182.

5. U.S. Congress, Senate, Finance Committee, Subcommittee on International Trade, Hearings before . . . , *Multinational Corporations* (Washington: G.P.O., 1973), pp. 1–2.

6. See chapter 5.

7. U.S. Congress, Senate, Finance Committee, Subcommittee on International Trade, Hearings before . . . , *Multinational Corporations*, pp. 276–278.

8. Ibid, pp. 302, 333–367.

9. Ibid., pp. 8–93, 193–224, 111–191, 243–275. The pagination reflects the sequence in which those testifying are mentioned in the text.

10. Ibid., pp. 299–301, quote on p. 299.

11. Ibid.

12. Ibid., pp. 300–301.

13. U.S. Congress, Senate, Committee on Foreign Relations, Subcommittee on Multinational Corporations, Hearings before . . . , *Multinational Corporations and U.S. Foreign Policy* (Washington: G.P.O., 1973), Part I and II and *CQA, 1973,* pp. 845–872.

14. U.S. Congress, Senate, Committee on Foreign Relations, Subcommittee on Multinational Corporations, Hearings before . . . , *Multinational Corporations and U.S. Foreign Policy*, Part I, p. 94.

15. Ibid., Part I, pp. 104, 114–115, and p. 261 for Church's quote.

16. *CQA, 1973*, pp. 845–852.

17. U.S. President, *International Economic Report of the President to Congress, 1973* (Washington: G.P.O., 1973), Appendix ix, pp. 130–131.

18. Ibid., pp. 1–94 passim.

19. Ibid., pp. 55–62, quoted material from p. 57.

20. For example, U.S. President, Commerce Department, Bureau of International Commerce, *The Multinational Corporation: Studies in Foreign Investment* (Washington: G.P.O., 1972–1973), I and II. These two volumes contain a total of five separate studies, four by various branches of the Commerce Department and one by the Conference Board, prepared at the request of the Secretary of Commerce.

21. U.S. Congress, House, Committee on Foreign Affairs, Subcommittee on Africa, Hearings before . . . , *U.S. Business Involvement in Southern Africa* (Washington: G.P.O., 1971), Part I, pp. 1–378 passim.

22. Ibid. (Washington: G.P.O., 1972), Part II.

23. Ibid. (Washington: G.P.O., 1973), Part III, pp. 1–239, passim, quote on p. 4 (emphasis added).

24. Ibid.

25. U.S. Congress, House, Committee on Foreign Affairs, Subcommittee on Foreign Economic Policy, Hearings before . . . , *The Overseas Private Investment Corporation* (Washington: G.P.O., 1973), pp. 1–432, quote on p. 1.

26. Ibid., *Report of the Subcommittee on Foreign Economic Policy: The Overseas Private Investment Corporation, October 21, 1973* (Washington: G.P.O., 1973), pp. 1–41.

27. U.S. Congress, Senate, Committee on Foreign Relations, Subcommittee on Multinational Corporations, Hearings before . . . , *Multinational Corporations and U.S. Foreign Policy: Overseas Private Investment Corporation, July–August, 1973* (Washington: G.P.O., 1973), pp. 1–651.

28. *Facts on File, 1973*, pp. 949–950 and *Congressional Information Service, Annual, 1974: Part 1, Abstracts* (Washington, DC: Congressional Information Service, 1975), p. 640.

29. U.S. Congress, House, Committee on Foreign Affairs, Study prepared for Congress by the Congressional Reference Service, *The Overseas Private Investment Corporation: A Critical Analysis* (Washington: G.P.O., 1973), pp. 1–107 passim.

30. U.S. Congress, Senate, Committee on Foreign Relations, Subcommittee on Multinational Corporations, Hearings before . . . , *Multinational Corporations and U.S. Foreign Policy: Overseas Private Investment Corporation* (Washington: G.P.O., 1973), Part III, pp. 1–651 passim.

31. *CQA, 1974,* pp. 519–525.

32. Ibid., pp. 520–521.

33. Chafe, *The Unfinished Journey,* pp. 420–421, quote on p. 421 and Kim McQuaid, *Big Business and Presidential Power: From FDR to Reagan* (New York: William Morrow & Co., Inc., 1982), pp. 282–283.

34. Conveniently, if somewhat dramatically, summarized by Anthony Sampson, *The Seven Sisters: The Great Oil Companies and the World They Shaped* (New York: Bantam Books, 1982), pp. 17–19, 297–300.

See also Robert Sherrill, *The Oil Follies of 1970–1980: How the Petroleum Industry Stole the Show* (New York: Anchor Press, 1983) and Walter S. Measday, "The Petroleum Industry," in *The Structure of American Industry,* ed. by Walter Adams (New York: Macmillan Publishing Co., 1982), pp. 38–39.

35. U.S. Congress, Senate, Committee on Foreign Relations, Subcommittee on Multinational Corporations, Hearings before . . . , *Multinational Corporations and U.S. Foreign Policy: Multinational Petroleum Companies and Foreign Policy* (Washington: G.P.O., 1974), Part V, pp. 1–73.

The summary of the negotiations between the London Policy Group and Lybia and the London Policy Group and the Gulf members of OPEC can be found in ibid., Part IV, pp. 75–98. It should be recognized that this summary reflects the oil companies' perspective.

36. Sampson, *The Seven Sisters,* pp. 316–325.

37. Ibid., p. 322.

38. Speech delivered in Iowa in December, 1973, and reprinted in U.S. Congress, Senate, Committee on Foreign Relations, Subcommittee on Multinational Corporations, Hearings before . . . , *Multinational Corporations and U.S. Foreign Policy: Multinational Petroleum Companies and Foreign Policy* (Washington: G.P.O., 1974), Part VIII, Appendix ix.

39. Ibid., *Multinational Oil Companies and U.S. Foreign Policy: Report, Together with Individual Views* (Washington: G.P.O., 1975), pp. 121–163.

40. Ibid., p. 16.

41. Ibid., Hearings before . . . , *Multinational Corporations and United States Foreign Policy: Multinational Petroleum Companies and Foreign Policy* (Washington: G.P.O., 1974–1975), Parts IV–IX.

42. Ibid., *Multinational Oil Corporations and U.S. Foreign Policy: Report Together with Individual Views,* conveniently summarized on pp. 151–155.

43. Ibid., pp. 155–156.

44. Ibid.

45. U.S. President, *International Economic Report of the President to Congress, 1974* (Washington: G.P.O., 1974), Part I and II.

46. Ibid., Part I, p. 16.

47. Ibid., Part II. Part II, while consisting of seven chapters, is still only 43 pages long.

48. U.S. Congress, Senate, Committee on Foreign Relations, Subcommittee on Multinational Corporations, Hearings before . . . , *Multinational Corporations and U.S. Foreign Policy: Multinational Petroleum Companies and Foreign Policy* (Washington: G.P.O., 1974), Part VII. Anderson's articles, reprinted from the *Washington Post,* are on pp. 470–478. Additional material, reflecting ARAMCO's response, can be found in ibid., Part VIII, Appendixes ii and iv.

49. Ibid., *Investments by Multinational Companies in the Communist Bloc Countries* (Washington: G.P.O., 1974), Part X. These hearings are placed in historical context by two staff studies prepared for the Subcommittee on Multinational Corporations. The first is an 83 page report, released on August 5, 1974, entitled *Western Investment in Communist Economies: A Selected Survey on Economic Interdependence* (Washington: G.P.O., 1974). The second is a 45 page report, released on December 20, 1974, entitled *U.S. Trade and Investment in the Soviet Union and Eastern Europe: The Role of the Multinational Corporation* (Washington: G.P.O., 1975).

7 THE "SECOND HALF OF WATERGATE": 1974–1978

President Nixon's conduct, the impeachment investigation, and his subsequent resignation confronted Gerald Ford with monumental political and constitutional problems that were rendered even more difficult by the unusual circumstances that had made him the Vice President.[1] It was therefore quite understandable that all the issues surrounding the phenomenon of corporate multinationalization suddenly seemed less urgent than these more basic problems.

The first document generated by the Ford administration that might have given some insight into its thinking on this subject was the legislatively-mandated annual *Economic Report of the President to Congress* released early in 1975. But, of necessity, this report had to focus on an immediate problem—a severe recession. It made any extended reference to the favorable or unfavorable consequences of corporate multinationalization wholly inappropriate.[2]

By March, 1975, however, things had changed. The defensive, catch-up atmosphere had passed, and Ford was beginning to define his own administration. In the covering letter for his first *International Economic Report of the President to Congress*, he characterized the global economic scene since 1971 as "turbulent" with the year under review, 1974, showing the effects of both inflation and recession. There was, he noted, an increase in the instances of expropriation of corporate assets, traceable in part to OPEC-inflated oil prices.[3] As was subsequently explained, the less-stable Third World countries sometimes expropriated the assets of multinational corporations and used the income derived from these business operations to purchase the oil needed to sustain their fragile economies. The problem of an increase in the instances of expropriation was cited as evidence of the instability in the international economy. Yet the losses experienced by the American firms apparently were not the administration's central concern. "We [i.e., the administration] . . . have taken steps to turn the difficult food, energy, trade, and *investment* issues into positive opportunities for achieving cooperation with trading partners and coordination between the nation's domestic and international economic policies."[4]

The actual report, written by the President's Council on International Economic Policy (CIEP) placed far greater emphasis on working within a cooperative economic climate than assessing the record of the year under review. There were frequent references to "consensus" statements, bilateral and multilateral "approaches," the "coordination" of efforts, and the various "exchanges" that had taken place between "interested" or "affected" parties. As a written document, it was more global in its orientation than its predecessor.[5]

It was within this context that the CIEP set forth the government's current policy toward expropriation. In many respects the policy statement was little more than a summary of past practices, yet by drawing together the disparate strands of past policy it became a fairly explicit statement of what the U.S. government would do to assist multinational corporations that were confronted with the expropriation or nationalization of their facilities by Third World countries needing revenue to purchase oil at OPEC-inflated prices.[6]

Furthermore, this *International Economic Report* permitted American multinational corporations to conclude that the Federal government had an identifiable expropriation policy that it wished to see codified in bilateral and multilateral agreements. Given the increase in the number of instances of expropriation over the preceeding twelve to fifteen months, it also suggested that the Federal government was still sensitive to the needs of American multinational enterprises. Conversely, it also had to be read as an endorsement of the proposition that the movement of capital, management, and technology to other countries should never be restricted except by market conditions.

A reiteration of the government's belief in the basic soundness and adequacy of the existing antitrust laws coupled with a stated preference for seeing antitrust questions resolved at a national rather than at an international level was also implicit in the report. It was an approach most multinational corporations, knowing the malleable nature of American antitrust policy, considered less menacing than defending their policies before some international tribunal.[7]

But the Congressional scene was a different matter. During the last week in February, 1974, Senator Frank Church, the aggressive and politically astute Chairman of the Senate's Subcommittee on Multinational Corporations, dropped a bombshell on the American public, currently taking some comfort in an OPEC-announced nine-month price freeze on its oil. Church announced that the Arab League, formed in 1945 to give political expression to the postwar aspirations of Arab nations, maintained a boycott list of some 1,500 American corporations because they either bought from or sold to Israel. The companies on the list, many of them multinational corporations, were presumably denied access to Arab markets that were now obviously flush with oil revenues thanks to the tactics of OPEC. Church noted that the boycott had been in place since 1946, but the number of companies on the list and the vigor with which the boycott was being enforced had increased considerably in recent months.

Church's announcement was accompanied by the release of what he identified as the Saudi Arabian "black list." He stated that the Subcommittee on Multinational Corporations would immediately initiate an investigation to determine if the Saudi government was imposing a pattern of "anti-Semitism upon our own business life," and whether the State Department and the Army Corp of Engineers, as the contracting agents for several Saudi projects, were acquiescing in this boycott. The list, released dramatically on February 26, 1974, included such high profile multinational enterprises as Ford, Xerox, RCA, and Coca Cola, all of whom, Church suggested, had been denied free access to Arab markets.[8]

Multinational corporations, long accustomed to being kept out of certain markets because of political considerations, had lived with these restrictions for some time, weighing the benefits of a vigorous Israeli market against the uncertainties of a usually smaller Arab market. As multinational enterprises they saw little difference between a minimally enforced Arab boycott against Israel and a more strictly enforced American boycott against trading with the Communist bloc countries of Eastern Europe. From their point of view, a boycott was a boycott.

Undoubtedly Church's motives were partially political; yet he did expose an interesting facet of government-corporate relations. Was the government of the United States, specifically the State Department and the Army Corp of Engineers, currying the favor of Saudi Arabia for diplomatic or strategic reasons? The hearings were brief but instructive. The witness for the Army Corp of Engineers, the deputy director for military construction, admitted excluding Jews from the Corp personnel assigned to Saudi Arabia and hedged on the procedure it used for choosing U.S. contractors and advising them on the use of employees of Jewish extraction in that country. The State Department's deputy assistant secretary for Near Eastern and South Asian affairs insisted the Arab boycott was anti-Zionist rather than anti-Semitic and explained that in any case the State Department was not "cooperating with it." The Treasury Department sent an assistant secretary to the hearings who advised the subcommittee of the existence of a U.S.-Arabian joint commission on Saudi Arabian investments in the United States and indicated that U.S. opposition to a boycott might be more forcefully expressed within the framework of this joint commission.[9]

The three days of testimony before the subcommittee were of greater concern to the Jewish community than they were to the corporate community. The latter expected few tangible returns from these and related hearings, and they were practical enough to realize that there were many things in this world that they could not change. President Ford's regulations of November 20, 1974 (effective December 1), preventing U.S. exporters and contractors from discriminating against U.S. citizens in response to foreign boycotts, were not expected to produce any significant changes in business practices. He also directed that all departments and agencies of the Federal government were to make foreign duty assignments on the basis of merit rather than the exclusionary policies of the host country.[10]

But there was a more substantive crisis confronting the multinational corporation at this time, one that it had no desire to see paraded before a congressional committee or dissected by the various news media for the benefit of the general public. The Watergate hearings and the subsequent investigations of the government's Special Prosecutor in the Watergate affair had established that some major American corporations had made numerous illegal or questionable political payments to public figures in the United States and abroad. George Steinbrenner's April, 1974 indictment on felony charges in connection with his allegedly illegal political contributions on behalf of his American Shipbuilding Corporation was only the tip of the iceberg. His high visibility as the new outspoken owner of the New York Yankees baseball team only made his indictment a more pressing ethical issue in the eyes of critical public interest groups.[11]

Campaign contributions had always been an integral part of the American political system, seldom praised, frequently excused, but regularly explained as something that "someday" would be eliminated, once the United States found a way of adequately financing election campaigns with tax dollars. This loosely constructed defense of the *status quo* suddenly seemed inadequate as the number of major corporations publicly acknowledging payments to elected or appointed public officials multiplied. By the early months of 1975, it was known that a substantial number of American companies had made contributions to elected officials to achieve specific corporate objectives. The fact that such payments were made "off the companies' financial records" and even, in some instances, without the knowledge of their board of directors further compromised the image of the companies involved. It came as no surprise that a former chairman of the Securities and Exchange Commission (SEC), Ray Garrett, Jr., called it "the second half of Watergate and by far the largest half."[12] But these numerous examples of corporate misconduct in domestic political affairs were soon overshadowed by glaring instances of massive corporate bribes of foreign officials to influence the policies of other countries.

Two congressional subcommittees responded almost immediately with investigations. The first to move was Church's well-staffed Subcommittee on Multinational Corporations. In May of 1975 it agreed to look into the foreign policy consequences of "offshore payments" to foreign officials, foreign governments, and the political parties of other countries. The subcommittee's basic justification for the investigation was the very damaging information that had surfaced as a result of the Watergate hearings. But they also had data released by the Securities and Exchange Commission, which established that several multinational corporations, some of them well known, had failed to report to their stockholders millions of dollars of "offshore payments," a clear violation of America's existing securities laws.[13]

The second subcommittee to open an investigation was the Subcommittee on International Economic Policy, a subcommittee of the House of Representatives' Committee on International Relations. It indicated that it intended to call representatives of the various government departments that had oversight responsibilities with respect to the activities of corporate America.[14] The effort of these two subcommittees, soon joined by other congressional or agency investigations, signaled the opening of a major inquiry into the use of corporate funds to secure favors or concessions in both foreign and domestic marketing operations.

The way the House's Subcommittee on International Economic Policy approached the issue dramatically documented the fundamental problems associated with the government's monitoring of business practices. To find out how the government investigated questionable or illegal payments and what its policies were if evidence of wrongful conduct was established, the subcommittee summoned officials from OPIC, the State Department, the IRS, the SEC, the Civil Aeronautics Board, and the Departments of Justice, Defense, and the Treasury. The number of agencies or departments testifying before this subcommittee became a virtual admission that the Federal government had no locus of governmental oversight responsibility when it came to monitoring the practices of corporate America. The actual testimony exposed conflicting jurisdictions, suggested conflicting objectives, and raised serious questions as to how far the Federal government should, or even could, go in monitoring the activities of any American enterprise in a foreign country. There were suggestions as to the need for more legislation, balanced against testimony that certain existing laws were already interfering with the basic mandate or function of other Federal agencies.[15]

But these hearings did not capture the headlines. It was Church's Subcommittee on Multinational Corporations that graphically revealed the depth of the ethical problems confronting the nation. Church, instead of focusing on the multiple agencies or departments of the government bureaucracy and how they functioned, called in the corporate executives of the companies that had made foreign payoffs an integral part of their overseas operations.

The first major company to be investigated by Church's subcommittee was the Northrop Corporation. The Northrop Corporation was not a multinational: as an aerospace "industry" that had massive military contracts with the Federal government, it was barred by law from maintaining foreign branches. Yet it did have substantial foreign markets for its aircraft. Apparently many of these markets had been secured and maintained through the payment of sizeable sums to foreign officials or agents purchasing from Northrop and then reselling their aircraft or parts to client countries. The Northrop hearings served to publicize a 530 page audit prepared by the accounting firm of Ernst & Ernst that was sprinkled with references to the "Lockheed arrangement," suggesting Northrop had adopted practices first employed by its competitor, the Lockheed Corporation, another aerospace industry that legally could not be a multinational corporation. The subcommittee, legitimately troubled over the foreign policy implications of foreign payoffs irrespective of whether the firm was or was not a multinational, expanded the scope of its inquiry.[16]

It was the Lockheed phase of the subcommittee's investigation that produced the most blatant examples of unethical practices. The company ultimately admitted it had made "offshore payments" totaling $202 million over an eight year period to foreign agents, government officials, and political parties in several different countries to further the sale of their aircraft. The headline-catching story was the $1.1 million commission to Prince Bernhard of the Netherlands, Queen Juliana's husband, to promote the sale of Lockheed aircraft in his own country and elsewhere in Europe. But the most remarkable revelation to surface from this aspect of the subcommittee's investigation was the admission of a Lockheed executive that the company had paid an Arab agent a generous commission to get Saudi Arabia to buy the C-130 military transport plane at a time when Saudi Arabia was not interested in purchasing any kind of military transport plane. It was not a case of Lockheed trying to outmaneuver its competitors (it readily admitted it really had none for the C-130 transport); it was a case of trying to get an oil-rich country to buy something it didn't want in the first instance.[17]

All this became more shocking because the chairman of Lockheed, Daniel Haughton, when previously questioned by the subcommittee, had insisted: "I didn't do anything wrong" and "We did it playing the rules of the game as they were then." It was, he suggested, what you had to do to survive in the international market place. And, Haughton argued, if the subcommittee intended to draft legislation outlawing foreign bribes or commissions, it should make certain that the language of the law was broad enough to cover "our competitors." He further insisted that the Federal government would have to do something to "internationalize" any regulations it imposed on American corporations so that foreign corporations would not acquire an unfair advantage over American firms when it came to securing contracts. It was a valid if selfish concern until, under further questioning by the subcommittee, the details of the attempted C-130 transport sale to Saudi Arabia were revealed. That story inevitably undermined Haughton's credibility.[18]

What Lockheed and a host of other companies had done was illegal in virtually every country of the world, yet corporations—multinational or national in structure—regularly made payments to public officials, political parties, or even governments themselves to facilitate business in some sector of their foreign operations. The hearings, and the corporate disclosures that surrounded them, suggested that illegal payments ranged from those judged essential to a company's economic survival, such as the multinational oil companies' insistence on doing whatever was necessary to protect their source of oil, to payments that simply created a market where none existed, such as Lockheed's attempt to sell the C-130 transport to Saudi Arabia. Payments that were hidden through elaborate schemes for "laundering" the monies meant the companies knew full-well that what they were doing was illegal in the United States. But the grey zone, from the government's point of view, was disturbingly broad. If Exxon, for example, was compelled to pay "royalties" to Arab sheiks to protect its oil supply, was it also compelled to give millions to the Communist Party in Italy to protect its refineries and markets in case that party came to power in Italy?[19] The fact that there were no easy answers to these ethical and economic questions did not temper the criticism.

Initially corporate America advanced the "few rotten apples" theory, but as the number of corporate confessions increased, such an explanation rang hollow. By 1976, the number and variety of Congressional and Federal agency investigations, and increased public scrutiny, were exposing so many examples of questionable practices that the credibility of corporate America was being challenged by friend and foe alike. All companies that engaged in international trade (as opposed to direct foreign investments) were suddenly being characterized as "multinationals" and these multinationals apparently achieved their awesome size and staggering profits not by their superior management style but by repeating the sins of their forebears. In effect, they were being viewed as the modern day version of the robber barons of the late 19th century, an image that corporate America's most imaginative public relations departments could not deflect.

In March, 1976, the CIEP released the President's annual *International Economic Report* to Congress for the year 1975. It offered President Ford and his Council their first opportunity to react to the disclosures and place the revelations about foreign bribes and payoffs in the context of a general review of international economic policy. In his letter of transmittal to Congress, the President expressed his "distress over reports of corrupt practices" and noted that he had instructed members of his administration "to take steps to assure *multinationals* obey the law," seemingly converting the word "multinational" into a generic term for all companies that break the law.[20] Beyond this, there were only a few brief references to bribery.

The section of the *International Economic Report* dealing with multinational corporations *per se* summarized the role being played by the Federal government in drafting guidelines for such things as short-term capital movements, transfer pricing, harmonization of tax and accounting standards, limiting antitrust jurisdiction, and transfer of technology. It indicated that the guidelines were being prepared in cooperation with the OECD (Organization for Economic Cooperation and Development) and that this effort at drafting guidelines was expected to expand into a broader effort under U.N. auspices, as well as a separate initiative with the Organization of American States. These matters, however, predated the bribery issue and were, in the early months of 1976, of little interest to those seeking some insight into administration thinking on the more pressing subjects of foreign payoffs and illegal payments.[21]

With this latest *International Economic Report* offering no concrete proposals on illegal corporate practices, the Senate Banking, Housing, and Urban Affairs Committee, under the chairmanship of Senator William Proxmire, introduced legislation (March 12, 1976) outlawing corporate bribes.[22] While several Senate committees held hearings on two different versions of Proxmire's bill with considerable misgivings as to its appropriateness, individual senators and representatives indicated they felt the proposed legislation would place corporate America's foreign sales operations at a severe disadvantage. They pointed out that what we characterized as questionable or illegal payments were frequently considered by others to be unavoidable, even accepted business practices.[23] As drafted, Proxmire's bill empowered the SEC to bring criminal action against those who violated the bill's provisions, immediately raising serious questions as to whether the bill altered the original mandate of the SEC, which was to protect the interest of the investor, not enforce ethical standards on corporate marketing practices.[24]

It was September, 1976, before Proxmire's somewhat modified proposal came to a vote in the Senate. This version of the Proxmire bill, regularly referred to as Senate bill S3664, passed the Senate on

September 15 by a vote of 86-0. In an effort to bypass hearings on his bill by the House of Representatives, Proxmire tried to have Senate bill S3664 attached as a rider to a bill that had already passed the House and was awaiting consideration by the Senate. Under this procedure, Senate bill S3664 would be sent to the House of Representatives as a part of a bill that the House had previously approved. Proxmire's procedural motion required the unanimous consent of the Senate. His motion failed and the session ended before the House had an opportunity to consider Senate bill S3664 as a separate bill. It died with the adjournment of this session of the 94th Congress.[25] A partial explanation for the failure of Proxmire's measure may be found in the President's announcement that he intended to address the questionable or illegal payments issue shortly.

The first substantive move on the President's part had come in March, 1976, with the creation of a cabinet-level Task Force on Questionable Corporate Payments, terminology more reflective of reality than had been the case up to this point with the casual linkage of the words "bribery" and "multinational." The task force was chaired by the Secretary of Commerce and included four other cabinet officers, the Secretaries of State, Treasury, and Defense, and the Attorney General. Other members of the task force included the President's Special Representative for Trade Negotiations, the Director of the Office of Management and Budget, the Assistant to the President for Economic Affairs, the Assistant to the President for National Security Affairs, and the Executive Director of CIEP.[26] The composition of the task force further documented the unstructured nature of the government's relations with corporate America and even this cumbersome entity did not reflect all the agencies or cabinet departments that had responsibilities in this area.

It was decided, although not necessarily by this task force alone, that the administration would address the problem in three ways: (1) by seeing to it that the existing laws and regulations were effectively enforced; (2) by developing new legislation to supplement and correct existing legislation; and (3) by pursuing international initiatives necessary to support or complement these domestic efforts. Implementing the first point involved calling attention to the ongoing activities of the IRS, the Federal Trade Commission, the SEC, and the Antitrust Division of the Justice Department in this area. As for new legislation, in August, 1976, President Ford, acting on the recommendation of his task force, sent to Congress the Foreign

Payment Disclosure Act. It required "enterprises" and their foreign subsidiaries to report for public disclosure a broad class of payments made in connection with transactions involving foreign government agencies, or other official acts of foreign officials, for the commercial benefit of these enterprises. Inherent in the bill was the notion that disclosure would eliminate illegal payments and hopefully curtail questionable payments, leaving only such "payments" as were perceived to be legitimate. It was a clear recognition of the difficulties of drafting legislation on this matter.[27]

The third area of administration policy, pursuing international initiatives to complement our domestic policy, addressed the most nebulous aspects of the corporate payments issue. The President proposed initiating discussions in the United Nations on drafting an international agreement to curb illicit payments. In response to this request, the United Nation's Economic and Social Council set up a "Working Group" to plan for an international convention. GATT (General Agreement on Tariffs and Trade), a specialized agency of the United Nations, was also asked to take up the questionable payments issue and the United States also concluded bilateral agreements with the enforcement authorities in some twelve countries for exchanging information regarding specific cases.

At the national and international levels, the focus was primarily on disclosure. Only the OECD drafted voluntary guidelines for "multinational enterprises." And it should be noted that the procedural or substantive proposals that emanated from the Ford administration did not single out the multinational corporation for special attention. In Congress, the various legislative initiatives of the Senate and the House, none of which secured passage, focused almost exclusively on disclosure as a remedy, and the multinational corporation was not singled out for any distinctive treatment. The Foreign Payment Disclosure Act, the most visible initiative of the executive branch, was never acted on by Congress.[28]

The most obvious explanation for these essentially investigative and procedural activities, none of which resulted in major legislation during 1976, was the inability of either the executive or legislative branches to codify ethical conduct. 1976 was also an election year, and the Ford administration still did not have a viable recovery program in place, leaving the President open to attack on domestic economic issues. A Republican administration had no desire to make the corporate community one of its critics by sponsoring a bill that was perceived as hostile to business. Also, by November, 1976, the questionable payments issue had lost its newsworthiness. Corporate confessions had become so commonplace that they were being relegated to the back pages of national newspapers, and they no longer qualified for inclusion on network evening news programs.

The collective impact of this steady stream of disclosures ultimately left corporate America under siege. By the latter part of the '70s, "government oversight" translated into a flood of forms, reports, questionnaires, and technical regulations that seemed to transform many corporate headquarters into fact-gathering secretariates and emporiums of corporate lawyers reducing government jargon to its minimal meaning.[29]

As the Ford administration was about to leave office, a victim of Jimmy Carter's surprising popularity, it released its last *International Economic Report*. It had a chapter devoted to multinational corporations—Chapter 3 of 13. The chapter focused on the various initiatives of international bodies over the past year to establish "guidelines" and/or "codes of conduct." The language used in this chapter suggested a cautious approval of these efforts coupled with repeated references to this or that being voluntary or nondiscriminatory and suggestive of possible solutions. There was also a strong statement as to the obligation of all governments to cooperate in resolving problems arising from the conflicting requirements imposed on multinational enterprises by virtue of the fact that they were inevitably subject to the jurisdictions of more than one government. In taking note of the administration's role in the U.N.-sponsored Conference on International Economic Cooperation, the *International Economic Report* stated that the United States was emphasizing the benefits associated with direct foreign investments and the need for host governments in developing countries to provide a stable investment climate.

Chapter 3 also took note of the growing demands of many developing countries to gain control over the technological improvements that multinational companies introduced into their economies. This was a comparatively recent development, involving the deliberate institutionalization of the technology transfer process. However, this *International Economic Report* categorically rejected this approach, arguing that technology was usually privately owned and should transfer only through conventional patterns of international investment. Lastly, the chapter dealt with expropriation, outright or implicit, such as mandatory indigenousization. There was a fairly strong statement about the government's concern over an increase in the incidents of expropriation where the adequacy of the compensation was in dispute.[30]

The subjects considered within this chapter of the 1977 *International Economic Report* and the language used to describe America's position reinforced the report's basic proposition: "The United States believes that MNCs [multinational corporations] have made and should be encouraged to continue to make major contributions to world economic development."[31] While being supportive of corporate multinationalization, it seemed to focus on, if not wholly support, the efforts of international agencies to establish "guidelines," "codes of conduct," or simply collect information.[32]

Although the compilers of this report gave considerable attention to these international efforts, they tended to view them as parallel to national efforts, valuable only as improving the climate for international business. The outgoing administration seemed to assume that these efforts would never be the dominant focus of control, that national initiatives and bilateral and multilateral agreements between governments would always be more important.[33]

The business community did not view these international initiatives quite so casually. Initially, its concern was traceable to the efforts of the International Confederation of Free Trade Unions (ICFTU). The presumption was that, of the various international organizations enacting resolutions with respect to the conduct of the multinational corporation, only organized labor had the potential coercive power to effectively enforce its resolutions. Their instrument of enforcement was the general strike or some other selective form of work stoppage. The fact that it had never been used successfully and that the American labor movement—the United Automobile Workers excepted—was not a part of the ICFTU, did not lessen the concern in the boardrooms of America's multinational corporations. The ICFTU had been committed to taming business since the '30s; it now represented 115 non-Communist unions in 89 nations. The initiative of such an organization in drafting a "Charter of Trade Union Demands for Legislative Control of MNCs [multinational corporations]" concerned all multinational enterprises, not because the ICTFU was considered powerful, but because the "Charter" was considered the most detailed and thoughtful set of proposals yet drafted by any international organization to tighten control over the multinational corporation. It had been three-and-a-half years in preparation and, with its adoption by the World Congress of the ICTFU in Mexico in October, 1975, it became a kind of bench-mark document that could not be dismissed. The hope of the ICTFU, and the concern of American multinational corporations, was that international and regional government organizations would use it as a model.[34]

As of January, 1977, its influence on the efforts of the established international agencies that were reviewed in the Ford administration's last *International Economic Report* appear to have been minimal. To date, the initiatives of these international agencies reflected compromises over rival national interests rather than compliance with, or rejection of, a labor point of view.

All this offered little comfort to the internationally-oriented segment of corporate America. Concrete evidence of their collective concern was the changing role of the United States Chamber of Commerce. Long identified with promoting or discouraging any legislation that impacted its broad constituency, the Chamber suddenly began to take on a new role. As various international agencies began drafting guidelines for multinational corporations, the Chamber began publishing status reports on "International Organization Activities Affecting International Investments." As of January, 1977, they were monitoring the policies of the Organization for Economic Cooperation and Development, the U.N.'s Economic and Social Council, the United Nations' Conference on Trade and Development's *ad hoc* committee of government experts on restrictive business practices and its committee on transfer of technology, the International Labor Organization, the U.N.'s Industrial Development Organization, and the Organization of American States. Equally important, and reflective of the bribery and questionable payments disclosures of 1975–1976, the Chamber published an "Elements of Global Business Conduct for Possible Inclusion in Individual Company Statements." These elements were drafted by a Multinational Corporation Panel, established by the Chamber to aid multinational enterprises in creating "company guidelines for conducting business in an international setting." The elements fell into two broad areas, those that addressed the issues being raised by the various international monitoring organizations and those that might help the multinational improve its image in the host country. In effect, the Chamber of Commerce was promoting self-regulation and self-discipline to lessen the likelihood of stiffer mandatory regulations by national or international bodies.[35]

All multinational enterprises, American and foreign, realized they were being perceived as a problem, as a type of foreign direct investment that, by their very existence, brought them into conflict with national interests and accepted international economic priorities, such as currency stability or balanced trade patterns. Since World War II, American multinational corporations had developed in an atmosphere of government benevolence, engendered by mutual, or at least noncompetitive, interests. But all that began to change in the early '70s, first as a result of the disclosures associated with the Watergate hearings and then as a result of the bribery and questionable payments practices of hundreds of corporations.

For the multinational corporation, the most menacing initiatives of the mid-'70s appeared to be international rather than national, seemingly challenging the tacit noninterference policies of most developed countries. As the 1977 *International Economic Report* of the President suggested, the Ford administration was still on their side, at least to the point of not advocating a more specific set of mandatory "codes."[36] But it was a far different climate from the generally supportive posture of the '60s. And, if the literature of the Chamber of Commerce accurately reflected the concern in the business community about the regulatory climate among international agencies, multinational corporations were rapidly reaching the conclusion that they had no choice but to aggressively state their own case in the global arena without the visibly supportive role from their historic partner—the U.S. government.

But as the concern over the Arab boycott of companies trading with Israel revealed, the Federal government was not out of the picture completely. In the 94th Congress an attempt was made to include an antiboycott provision in a bill extending the life of the Export Administration Act of 1969. Because the Ford administration felt that the strictness of the provisions that had been written by both the Senate and House would prevent U.S. firms from participating in the trade boom in the Middle East and would jeopardize our diplomatic efforts to achieve peace in the region, the legislative effort of the 94th Congress failed. During the presidential campaign of 1976, the recently nominated candidate of the Democratic Party, Jimmy Carter, criticized Ford for opposing these congressionally sponsored antiboycott measures, suggesting a Democratic Party victory in November would prompt a Democratic-controlled Congress to sponsor a new antiboycott bill.[37]

Following the failure of the 94th Congress to include its antiboycott provisions in the bill extending the life of the Export Administration Act of 1969, an extraordinary round of negotiations was initiated among Jewish organizations, key U.S. industry leaders belonging to the Business Roundtable, members of Congress, and ultimately, members of the Carter administration. The main difficulty for Congress and the new administration was to write an antiboycott provision into the bill that would protect American business interests with the Arab states of the Middle East and still satisfy the demands of some of the important Jewish organizations in the United States.

By January 28, 1977, corporate executives belonging to the Business Roundtable and members of the Anti-Defamation League of B'nai B'rith were actively engaged in formulating a set of common principles on the boycott issue. They were openly and deliberately heavy-handed as lobbyists in their attempt to push through Congress a measure that would be acceptable to both the business community and Jewish groups in the United States. Their principles were made public in March and then, almost immediately, suffered a major setback when the coalition disagreed over the meaning of certain critical passages in the document itself. The conferees and their congressional supporters continued to meet to resolve their differences, ultimately working out a compromise that both houses of Congress could support. It allowed Arab states to specify the manufacturer of the more visible components of a product it was ordering, but not the less identifiable parts, so long as the request was not knowingly based on race, religion, sex, or the national origin of the manufacturer. President Carter put his signature on the compromise measure in June, 1977. It was a rare example of two essentially divergent interest groups constructing an essentially technical compromise to try and neutralize a boycott that had significant economic, emotional, and religious consequences.[38]

Two measures during 1977 demonstrated how dramatically the Federal government had distanced itself from the multinational corporation. In July, Congress completed action on a foreign economic aid bill for the 1978 fiscal year. What made this annual foreign aid ritual more worthy of note than the previous efforts of Congress was the complete removal of corporate America as an instrument of, or even a direct beneficiary of, our AID (Agency for International Development) program. As such, it represented a major shift in focus, from a "trickle-down" approach to a bill that provided for direct humanitarian assistance, with need being the prime criterion for aid. We had moved from the Marshall Plan conception of aid that was military and economic and, in effect, directed toward Western Europe, to a second phase, namely attempting to build the infrastructure of Third World countries so that they might share in the global economy, to an approach that, by 1977, was almost totally humanitarian in its budget allocation and distinctly bilateral in its approach. The shifting focus was the result of domestic budgetary constraints and altered circumstances in the international arena, but the net effect was to sever the most enduring link in the partnership between government and business in terms of America's global responsibilities since World War II. The signs had been there for several years, but the foreign aid package passed in 1977 has to be perceived as at least the first visible evidence of a severance of that partnership.[39]

A somewhat less significant sign of the changed climate was the failure of Congress to complete action on a bill to renew and expand OPIC. OPIC, created in 1969 with little support from the business community, had amassed a host of Congressional critics by 1974, in part because of ITT's apparent efforts to use its ties with OPIC to persuade the Federal government to intervene in Chile to protect its holdings from being expropriated by Salvador Allende. The current effort in 1977 to renew and expand OPIC (still without any significant involvement by the business community) was premised on the belief that at least much of the Congressional hostility toward the agency had diminished. Its supporters soon discovered that it had not. Confronted with amendments considered detrimental to the agency's viability, its advocates in Congress withdrew the bill from further consideration in hopes of having a more favorable climate for the renewal and enhancement of the agency's functions in 1978. For the corporate community, these Congressional initiatives were of little value; for them OPIC was a nonissue, politically controversial, and perceived as only marginally or selectively beneficial in Third World investment projects.[40]

Symbolically, at least, the partnership between the Federal government and the corporate community was dissolved with the passage of the Foreign Corrupt Practices Act of 1977. "For the first time in U.S. history it . . . [became] a crime for corporations to bribe an official of a foreign government or political party in order to obtain, or retain, business in another country."[41] The deliberate criminalization of illegal corporate payments represented the culmination of five years of debate over the appropriate response to the revelations about the various types of "corporate slush funds" used to obtain or retain a market advantage over competitors. The initial remedy, a simple "disclosure" to the SEC or some other agency of the Federal government of a payment that had been made in connection with a foreign business transaction or potential transaction, lost its credibility as some 400 corporations ultimately admitted making millions of dollars of illegal or questionable payments to foreign officials. Supporters of the criminalization approach, encouraged by the Carter administration, pushed through the legislation that, initially at least, left the business community in disarray. Under the terms of the act, a company, if convicted, was liable for fines of up to $1 million and individuals within the corporation (officers, directors, employees, or shareholders) could face maximum fines of $10,000, or up to five years imprisonment, or both. The act would generate endless debate over its real meaning but, minimally speaking, it was a dramatic manifestation of the negative climate toward the internationally-oriented business community in the mid-'70s.[42]

But it also has to be recognized that this negative climate of the mid-'70s was not created by the Federal government, but by corporate America and its own insensitivity to the minimal moral and ethical values expected of it by American society. While corporate America, and specifically its flamboyant standard-bearer, the multinational corporation, had its critics—labor, Blacks, environmentalists—its real enemy seems to have been the self-serving profit and power oriented professional managerial teams that were now defining the tone and temper of the business world.[43] Whether they realized it or not, they had given meaning and substance to the investigations of the Subcommittee on Multinational Corporations and its many congressional clones, and they were now forced to recognize that they must live with the consequences of their narrowly focused management style.

NOTES

1. On October 12, 1973, Ford, the House minority leader, was selected to replace Spiro Agnew as vice president after Agnew resigned that office.

2. U.S. President, *Economic Report of the President Transmitted to the Congress, 1975* (Washington: G.P.O., 1975), carries only a few casual references to multinational businesses and private foreign investments in its 229 pages.

3. U.S. President, *International Economic Report of the President Transmitted to the Congress, 1975* (Washington: G.P.O., 1975), p. iii.

4. Ibid.

5. Ibid., pp. 1–166.

6. Ibid., pp. 54–55.

7. Ibid., pp. 73–75.

8. U.S. Congress, Senate, Committee on Foreign Relations, Subcommittee on Multinational Corporations, Hearings before . . . , *Multinational Corporations and United States Foreign Policy: Political and Financial Consequences of the OPEC Price Increases* (Washington: G.P.O., 1975), Part XI, pp. 195–196. The Saudi Arabian "black list" is on pp. 371–476.

9. Ibid., pp. 195–196.

10. *Congressional Quarterly Almanac, 1975,* p. 344 (henceforth cited as *CQA*).

11. *Facts on File,* April 20, 1974, pp. 304–305.

12. Garrett's characterization of the climate in the mid-'70s was related to the author by George McKann, the late Mr. Garrett's co-counsel when the former SEC chairman was serving as an outside legal advisor to boards of directors concerned about "sensitive payments" problems in their own corporate structures. Mr. McKann said Garrett repeatedly reminded his clients and any other audience he could reach in the corporate community that what was happening was literally the "second half of Watergate."

13. U.S. Congress, Senate, Committee on Foreign Relations, Subcommittee on Multinational Corporations, Hearings before . . . , *Multinational Corporations and United States Foreign Policy: Political Contributions to Foreign Governments* (Washington: G.P.O., 1976), Part XII, pp. 1–1175. See opening statement of Senator Frank Church, ibid., pp. 1–2.

14. U.S. Congress, House, Committee on International Relations, Subcommittee on International Economic Policy, Hearings before . . . , *Activities of American Multinational Corporations Abroad* (Washington: G.P.O., 1975), pp. 1–330.

15. Ibid.

16. *CQA, 1975,* pp. 413–414.

U.S. Congress, Senate, Committee on Foreign Relations, Subcommittee on Multinational Corporations, Hearings before . . . , *Multinational Corporations and United States Foreign Policy: Political Contributions to Foreign Governments,* Part XII, pp. 395–449, 451–564, 565–683, 750–838.

17. Ibid., pp. 345–392, 935–1000 [Indonesia], 1001–1114 [Saudi Arabia], 1115–1139 [Iran], 1141–1171 [Philippines].

18. Ibid., pp. 345–392 for Haughton's testimony, quotes on pp. 356 and 346, respectively. See also ibid., Part XIV, pp. 1–452.

19. Ibid., Part XII, pp. 241–267. See also "Report on Special Audit and Investigation in Italy," Standard Oil Corporation (NJ), pp. 268–313.

20. U.S. President, *International Economic Report of the President . . . , 1976* (Washington: G.P.O., 1976) [letter of transmittal, pages unnumbered].

21. Ibid., pp. 50, 80–84.

22. U.S. Congress, Senate, Committee on Banking, Housing, and Urban Affairs, Hearings before . . . , *Foreign and Corporate Bribes* (Washington: G.P.O., 1976), pp. 1–119.

23. *CQA, 1976,* pp. 244–247.

24. U.S. Congress, Senate, Committee on Banking, Housing, and Urban Affairs, Hearings before . . . , *Foreign and Corporate Bribes,* pp. 2–3. Proxmire's bill sought to amend the Securities and Exchange Act of 1934.

25. *CQA, 1976,* pp. 244–247.

26. Ibid. and U.S. President, *International Economic Report of the Presi-*

dent..., *1977* (Washington: G.P.O., 1977), pp. 50–51, 69–72. The report also summarizes what the administration had done during 1976.

27. U.S. President, *International Economic Report of the President...*, *1977*, pp. 69–72.

28. Ibid.; *CQA, 1976*, pp. 244–247, 257–264.

29. The structure and scope of Grover Starling's *The Changing Environment of Business: A Managerial Approach* (Boston: Kent Publishing Co., 1980) dramatically documents the appropriate managerial focus and areas of competence seemingly required of individuals in the late '70s. It has chapters or subsections dealing with "social responsibility," "applied ethics," "governmental actions on environmental quality," "equal employment opportunity," "occupational safety and health," "why business gets involved in the political process," "political action and electoral activities," "government activities," and "politics is every manager's concern."

30. U.S. President, *International Economic Report of the President...*, 1977, p. 51. Chapter 3 is pp. 69–72.

31. Ibid., p. 69.

32. Ibid., pp. 69–72.

33. Ibid., pp. 1–128.

34. Burton Binder, *International Labour Affairs: The World Trade Unions, and the Multinational Companies* (Oxford, England: The Clarendon Press, 1987), pp. 34–65, 90, 103–105, 112–113, 150–153.

For background and context see Harold B. Malmgren, "International Organizations in the Field of Trade and Investment," in *United States International Economic Policy in an Interdependent World* (Washington: G.P.O., 1971), II, pp. 427–449 and John Robinson, *Multinationals and Political Control* (New York: St. Martin's Press, 1983), pp. 103–104, 145–146, 153, 274–282.

35. Reported on in U.S. Congress, House, Committee on Banking, Currency, and Housing, Subcommittee on International Trade, Investment, and Monetary Policy, report prepared by the staff of the subcommittee . . . , *International Investment Uncertainty* (Washington: G.P.O., 1977), pp. 57–58.

36. U.S. President, *International Economic Report of the President...*, *1977*, pp. 69–70.

37. *CQA, 1976*, pp. 257–264.

38. *CQA, 1977*, pp. 352–359.

39. Ibid., pp. 359–363. A foreign military aid bill for the Middle East and North Africa cleared Congress at about the same time and its provisions obviously benefitted the defense and aerospace sectors of the corporate world.

40. Ibid., pp. 390–392.

41. Starling, *The Changing Environment of Business*, p. 174.

42. CQA, 1977, pp. 413–414.

See U.S. Congress, Senate, Committee on Banking, Housing, and Urban Affairs, Hearings before . . . , *Foreign and Corporate Bribes* (Washington: G.P.O., 1976), pp. 1–119; ibid., *Foreign Corrupt Practices and Domestic and Foreign Investment Disclosures* (Washington: G.P.O., 1977), pp. 1–245.

See also *Facts on File, 1977*, pp. 937–938 and a highly critical analysis of the whole question by Neil H. Jacoby, Peter Nehemkis, and Richard Eells, *Bribery and Extortion in World Business: A Study of Corporate Political Payments Abroad* (New York: Macmillan Publishing Co., Inc., 1977), pp. 1–276.

43. Starling, *The Changing Environment of Business*, gives voice to what is needed to correct the prevailing outlook of those in management: "Today [1980] the need is for leaders who, through their own example, will raise business [sic] and other managers to new possibilities and who have the ability and will to take positions that clearly embody the public interest" (p. 582).

See also Alfred D. Chandler, Jr., *The Visible Hand: The Managerial Revolution in American Business* (Cambridge: Harvard University Press, 1977), and the more recent study by Louis Galambos and Joseph Pratt, *The Rise of the Corporate Commonwealth: United States Business and Public Policy in the 20th Century* (New York: Basic Books, 1988).

8 A NEW TOLERANCE AND THE FADING OF THE PARTNERSHIP: THE YEARS AFTER 1977

By the time the Federal Corrupt Practices Act became law in December of 1977, thirteen months after Jimmy Carter was elected President, the list of corporations that had already "confessed" to foreign bribes and payoffs had reached staggering proportions. Most of them were multinational firms, suggesting an even more hostile climate for these economic behemoths than prevailed during the previous four years. It was also feared that a thoughtfully ethical President with a strong commitment to Christian values would convert this act into a crusade against the kinds of activities that had been exposed in the investigative atmosphere that prevailed in Washington after Watergate. Carter came to Washington as an outsider and after one year in office he seemed determined to stay that way. His was the perfect mind set for making corporate America pay for its "sins," yet that is not what happened. The President discovered that, not only campaign promises but his deeply felt convictions had to bend to reality.

As Carter began his second year in office, the recession that had plagued the Ford administration seemed to be over, permitting him to give the country a more "efficient" and a more "competent" government as he had promised in his inaugural address the previous year. But as his first annual economic report to Congress in January, 1978, candidly admitted, there were still troubling remnants of the recession. Unemployment was still too high and inflation seemed to be "stuck" at about 6 percent. These were conditions that were traditionally unacceptable to any Democratic administration and particularly so to this one, that came into office with a mixed constituency. Carter's economic advisors were also acutely aware of other troubling characteristics in the recovering economy.[1] Business simply did not trust the recovery and refused to make new capital investments. And, the economic indicators suggested they were right in their assessment. In fact, there were even signs that the recovery was losing its momentum.

By April, 1978, Carter was forced to change the focus of his economic policy, giving a higher priority to fighting inflation because it was being perceived as the most serious obstacle to a sustained recovery. He promised the business community that he would not resort to wage-price controls, asking, in return, that both business and labor voluntarily try to keep wages and prices below the rate of increases of the previous two years. It was Carter's first public effort to win the support of the business community, which, he had come to realize, he needed if his political and economic goals were to be achieved.[2] There was also a disturbing development in the international monetary markets—a glut of dollars, particularly in Europe, as a result of a greater volume of U.S. imports over its exports. The trade imbalance had caused the dollar to drop in value against foreign currencies, potentially destabilizing the money market. And foreigners, like Americans, came to realize that America's seemingly unmanageable inflation was eroding the value of the dollar even further.[3]

With a troubled domestic economy and a potentially serious international monetary crisis, corporate image bashing did not seem appropriate. Not surprisingly, the Federal Corrupt Practices Act of 1977 lost its urgency. Within the corporate community this effort to legislate morality had only served to generate massively detailed oversight procedures and numerous and impossibly ambiguous "ethical guidelines," all emanating from corporate headquarters for the guidance of those individuals or branch offices that handled foreign contracts.[4] But that was virtually all the act generated.

As far as the Carter administration was concerned, by 1978 foreign corrupt practices by businesses had become a nonissue. Quite simply, the White House decided it needed a more vigorous economy to help solve its inflationary pressures and control its international monetary and balance of payments problems. Within a matter of months, the

Justice Department and the SEC began to "look the other way," and by July, 1978, the Justice Department's task force monitoring foreign payoffs was candidly admitting to the *Wall Street Journal* that it was currently investigating "roughly a dozen matters" involving *possible* illegal payments by U.S. companies.[5] It was information that surprised no one in the corporate community, given the fact that the previous month the *New York Times* had run a front page story headlined "U.S. Law Against Bribes Blamed for Millions of Lost Sales in Asia."[6] And quite independent of the less than enthusiastic enforcement practices in Washington, it was widely believed that knowledgeable corporate managers operating abroad already knew how to circumvent the law if the transaction seemed profitable and comparatively risk-free.[7]

Congress-watchers within the business community had already discovered that the legislative branch had lost much of its passion for the Federal Corrupt Practices Act. In fact, the business community had some hard evidence in the handling of a bill to extend the life of OPIC to back up their conviction. The operating authority of OPIC had been allowed to lapse on December 31, 1977, because many members of the House of Representatives had been reluctant to support the agency during the previous legislative session.

Recognizing the short-sightedness of their action, the House, in February, 1978, passed a bill extending the agency's life. The House bill was virtually identical to a bill that had been passed by the Senate in the closing weeks of its session in 1977. A Senate-House conference committee met to resolve the technical differences between the two bills. The most interesting aspect of this largely procedural legislative activity was that one of the technical differences between the House and Senate bills was a provision in the House bill that denied the claims of investors who were "convicted" of bribing a foreign official in connection with an OPIC-insured project. The Senate bill, by contrast, said nothing about bribery negating a claim payment.

In the House-Senate conference committee report, the more stringent House provision was deleted in favor of a clause that stated that claims would be denied if it was found that bribery was the "preponderant cause" of the loss. Practically speaking, Congress, in extending the life of OPIC (admittedly only an option for business) through September 30, 1992, backed away from using it as an instrument for showcasing the Federal Corrupt Practices Act in the underdeveloped areas of the world.[8]

In July, 1978, the Bonn Economic Summit brought the heads of the seven major industrial nations of the world together amidst predictions that they would be unable to effectively deal with the current international economic problems—the disturbing mix of inflation, recession, and unemployment or, as it was being called, "stagflation." The modest efforts agreed upon at the Bonn Summit to help combat worldwide unemployment without rekindling the inflationary patterns of the previous few years were far from reassuring.[9]

What seemed to be happening at Bonn was but a pale reflection of what was happening generally in international economic developments. U.S. dominance of global economic patterns, like U.S. military dominance, was fading, regardless of who occupied the White House. The United States no longer wrote the script for these economic summits and corporate America, and specifically the American multinational corporation, was no longer the private sector's most vigorous economic force in global economic developments. Foreign multinational enterprises now shared the spotlight as a "cheaper" dollar generated growing capital investments *in* the United States rather than the pattern we had come to take for granted, namely, capital investments *by* the United States. Those who monitored international economic developments realized that this was something that had been happening since the early '70s, but it had been gradual, and few in Washington paid much attention to it. It was not until OPEC countries began recycling their considerable oil profits into the global economy that both developed and underdeveloped countries began to take note of the realignments that were taking place in foreign investment patterns.[10]

It was these new investment patterns that led to the development of a new mode of foreign investment, what was being called "unbundling." In the past, multinational enterprises, and particularly American firms, usually established wholly-owned subsidiaries in the Third World markets that they judged profitable. Now both economic and political considerations were forcing them to "unbundle" their services, to provide one or possibly two specific services in some form of partnership arrangement either with a domestic enterprise in the market area they sought to penetrate or even with the government itself in certain situations. These various arrangements would ultimately be classified as "joint ventures."

The American multinational corporation soon discovered that as OPEC profits were transferred to the international financial markets, an alternate source of investment capital become available to local companies or governments in "underdeveloped" areas, reducing the need of these Third World companies or governments to depend on the American multinational corporation to supply all the elements of the free enterprise system—capital, technology, and management. Instead, these Third World companies or governments elected to borrow money from international banks flush with the deposits of the OPEC countries and then buy specific services from multinational enterprises through contractual arrangements that made the multinational firm a subordinate partner in a joint venture rather than the sole owner of the facility. These developments served to make multinational enterprises a less visible target for critics both at home and abroad. Joint ventures seemed to blend into the economic landscape of the developing country, becoming part of an amorphous group of firms that were loosely characterized as "local corporations with foreign interests."[11]

In May of 1979, *New York Times* columnist Russell Baker saw fit to ask rhetorically, "How's Business?" His freewheeling and typically outrageous answer suggested that in terms of the venerable and much abused "national state," things were not too good; but if one was referring to the "state's" economic counterpart, the multinational corporation, they were doing perfectly fine. If, Baker suggested, multinational firms could just keep national states in business for the purpose of performing all the unproductive chores of modern society, such as maintaining an "atomic arsenal" or defending to the death their multiple and hopelessly outdated ideologies, there was no limit to the potential of the multinational corporation itself. For the indefatigable author of the "Sunday Observer" column, the multinational firm was clearly the peerless defender of the world's perpetual quest for the "good life," supplying everything from oil to "stomach carbonization," i.e., Coke and Pepsi for "thirsty Communists." With his droll absurdities, Russell Baker gave credence to the notion that corporate multinationalism had become one of the less frightening anomalies of the 20th century. It was a problem, but it was no longer as worrysome as the Ethiopian famine, Middle East terrorism, or the latest cancer statistics, subjects nobody dared trivialize.[12]

The fact was, the traditional fears about corporate multinationals dominating the national state and controlling the international economy had given way to more specific concerns, suggesting a growing willingness to view multinational enterprises as an essential part of the fabric of the international economy, not only in the "free world" and in "developing" or "Third World" countries, but even (to use a fourth category found in United Nations studies) in the "socialist countries of eastern Europe."[13]

Meanwhile, President Carter, still troubled by the unresolved economic problems facing the nation, had turned his attention to defusing the Israeli—Egyptian issue, hoping to make the oil-rich Middle East somewhat less volatile. His efforts bore fruit in terms of the Camp David Agreements, signed on September 17, 1978, suggesting that perhaps Carter was not as ineffectual as many had come to believe.

For its part, Congress was becoming marginally concerned about foreign investments *in* the United States, at least to the extent that it affected ownership of America's farm land. In response to the pleas of American farmers, Congress drafted legislation requiring foreign or domestic corporations or individuals who purchased farm land to report their purchases to the Secretary of Agriculture. The reporting requirement became the first explicit deviation from our traditional laissez-faire attitude toward foreign investments *in* the United States.[14] Otherwise, Congress virtually ignored the corrupt practices issue during the Carter administration, even though the continued disclosures of past foreign payoffs by American corporations doing business internationally were being regularly reported—in a nonaccusatory manner—on the inner pages of the *Wall Street Journal*.[15]

By 1979, the focus had shifted from enforcing the Federal Corrupt Practices Act to a debate on whether it was more appropriate for the Justice Department or the SEC to draft guidelines for businesses so they would not run afoul of the act. Since its passage in December of 1977, the business community had lobbied hard, principally through the Commerce Department, to get the SEC and/or the Justice Department or some Federal agency or department to either issue guidelines or seek the repeal of the act.[16] The law, corporate executives insisted, was not only hopelessly ambiguous, but was certain to result in the loss of overseas contracts where payoffs were intrinisic to business transactions, which, in turn, would inevitably worsen the trade balance.

For several months the SEC and the Justice and Commerce Departments had been arguing over the practical and ethical implications of issuing guidelines, with the strongest opposition coming from the SEC. The chief of its enforcement division, Stanley Sporkin, bluntly told the *New York Times*: "We don't have guidelines for rapists, muggers, and embezzlers, and I don't think we need guidelines for corporations who want to bribe foreign officials."[17] But President Carter and his economic advisors had to face a different reality.

In November, 1978, the President had taken a series of corrective measures through the Treasury Department to bolster the dollar on the world money markets. He also created an Export Disincentives Task Force to study ways of improving the U.S. trade balance by removing what he characterized as "roadblocks" to American exports. To implement the removal of one of these perceived roadblocks, he specifically instructed the Justice Department to clarify the Federal Corrupt Practices Act as part of a general effort to increase American exports over imports. This request was the first hard evidence that Carter was responding to the growing trade deficit and pressure from the business community on this specific piece of legislation. It was a directive that cleared the way for change.[18]

Early in June, 1979, the Export Disincentives Task Force explicitly recommended that:

The Justice Department, by next September, should issue written guidance to the business community about the law, including establishment of enforcement priorities, discussion of hypothetical situations and creation of a business review procedure by which corporations could get advance Government reaction to specific overseas payoff plans.

The Administration should consider the feasibility of amending the law, "to take enforcement responsibilities away from the SEC. . . ."

The Administration should periodically inform Congress and the public about the export losses caused by the law. This could pave the way for seeking modifications in that law that would "permit U.S. companies to be guided by the laws of the foreign countries where they do business."[19]

As the *New York Times* observed on June 17, 1979, "the simple imperatives of morality in business conduct have been complicated by other forces, including antiregulatory sentiments, economic exigencies, and foreign policy considerations."[20] Reality was catching up with the Carter administration.

As 1979 drew to a close, the problems in our domestic economy remained every bit as worrisome as they had been when Carter delivered his second economic report to Congress the previous January. At midyear, OPEC had announced another round of price increases, virtually guaranteeing another year of economic problems for all nations dependent on Middle East oil. In July, the price of gold rose to over $300 per ounce on the London market, and by December it had passed the $500 per ounce figure in New York, a sign that few expected a stable economic climate in the '80s. In November, the followers of Ayatollah Khomeini seized the U.S. embassy in Tehran, taking sixty-two Americans as hostages. Not only had the State Department and the CIA seemingly misjudged the political climate in Iran, but the positive accomplishments that appeared to flow from the Camp David Agreements were virtually forgotten as another small, fanatically driven, nation humiliated the United States. In this climate the ethical standards of multinational enterprises, or any other corporate entity for that matter, were rather unimportant.

In Congress there were intermittent hearings by the Judiciary Committee's Subcommittee on Antitrust, Monopoly, and Business Rights to consider amending the Clayton Antitrust Act of 1914 to prohibit mergers and acquisitions by corporations with assets or sales in excess of $2 billion. This obviously included multinational corporations that fell within the subcommittee's description. The hearings shifted briefly to proposals to restrict oil companies, awash with huge profits, from acquiring companies outside the petroleum sector. The intent in this case was to force multinational oil companies to use their profits to find new domestic sources of oil rather than diversify into other profitable and less capital-intensive ventures. The subcommittee also considered proposals restricting the acquisition of family farms by large nonfarming domestic or foreign investors seeking diversification.[21] The hearings generated no major legislative proposals and their disjointed specificity isolated them from the mainstream of economic policy formation. Moreover, there was nothing in the tone of these hearings to suggest that corporate multinationals were again the target of a major Congressional investigation.

In fact, multinational corporations were no longer a central concern of either the executive or legislative branch of government. The most recent annual economic reports of President Carter barely mentioned them, and Congress virtually ignored them.[22]

An important reason for this growing disinterest was a shattering of their image of invincibility. The government's hasty bailout of the financially troubled Chrysler Corporation in December, 1979, was high drama in the historic debate over whether the multinational corporation or the Federal government was the more powerful force in American society. The so-called "Chrysler rescue" actually proved nothing about the strength or resilience of the American multinational corporation, yet in the public mind, and even within some influential sectors of the Federal bureaucracy, the apparent helplessness of Chrysler suggested that many of the fears of the previous decades about the awesome power of multinational firms were unfounded.[23]

The confrontational climate of the pre-1977 years had receded so dramatically—literally evaporated—that it was almost impossible to detect. Even the AFL-CIO, uncertain of its own strength in a troubled domestic economy, seemed to be more willing to once again tolerate some form of corporate multinationalism as an inevitable component of the international economy. All sides—government, business, and labor—apparently assumed that an accommodation of interests was the only rational way of living in the complex and interdependent international economic climate that seemed to be the hallmark of the late '70s and the decade of the '80s.

Much of the Federal government's tolerance of the practices of multinational corporations can be traced to a changed emphasis on which business activities or practices Washington should monitor. For several years, both the state and Federal governments had been under pressure to address problems that had a social rather than an essentially market-related impact. Issues such as environmental hazards, discriminatory employment practices toward women, Blacks, and Latinos, and unhealthy or dangerous working conditions that threatened the lives or health of workers were perceived as more worthy of attention than technical violations of our frequently cited antitrust laws or questionable business practices in securing foreign markets. Broad-based regulations to correct these "fundamental" social problems generally touched all sectors of the business community and the category "multinational" became a less meaningful term with the agencies or departments enforcing these regulations. And it should be recognized that the Federal agencies most active in these areas were addressing problems that had nothing to do with size or global influence.

The uncompromising attitude of the committed environmentalists or zealous human rights activists who administered these agencies annoyed many in the business community, and they did not disguise their impatience with what they considered the unrealistic agenda of these reformers. Some business leaders did whatever they could to weaken, deflect, or resist any regulation that was, in their judgement, economically imprudent. Yet, since the practices being outlawed or the safety regulations being imposed did not pivot on a particular corporate structure, it was not construed as an attack on multinational corporations *per se*. In fact, the larger corporations, including multinational enterprises, usually had the necessary economic resources and sense of public image to comply more readily with these regulations than the smaller businesses with limited economic resources trying to survive in an inflation-plagued economy.

Aside from these factors, there was another dimension to American corporate expansion outside of the United States that influenced the ever-changing relationship between the Federal government and the multinational corporation. From the immediate postwar years up to the early '70s, the U.S. government had taken a rather skeptical view of international or regional agencies attempting to regulate multinational enterprises. Initially these regulatory efforts were generated by the various permanent monitoring councils of the United Nations or by regional organizations. The American response was usually a quiet and polite opposition by our staff professionals at our U.N. mission or through the appropriate embassy. Most industrialized countries of the West shared this attitude. However, as the international economy became more complex, bilateral or multilateral consultations on problems involving the practices of multinational firms became more frequent.

Historically, both the Federal government and the American multinational corporation premised their policies on a firm commitment to a free-market economy. The global or regional "guidelines" or "codes of conduct" that were drafted by the various international or regional agencies concerned with the practices of multinational firms did not directly challenge this philosophy, but the tendency toward drafting ground rules did require the constant monitoring of the agencies involved so that they might be persuaded not to adopt an adversarial posture toward corporate multinationalism. Each successive administration in Washington worked instinctively to prevent these multilateral talks from generating invasive policies that were perceived as infringing on the investment strategies of the American multinational corporation.[24]

Then, in the late '70s and early '80s, as the international economy deteriorated, these agencies inevitably became more aggressive, anxious to create a more stable investment climate through international controls of multinational firms. Of all the industrialized countries of the West, probably the United States had the least faith in international controls. Yet, to the extent that the other industrialized countries, particularly our major trading partners within the OECD (Organization for Economic Cooperation and Development), saw such international efforts as useful or inevitable, the United States reluctantly went along with the less-invasive controls. The result was an ever-expanding web of international or regional monitoring organizations that imposed real or psychological restraints on many of the activities of all multinational corporations.[25]

A far more serious threat to the laissez-faire attitude that was the hallmark of American policy was the economic agenda of the Group of 77—a powerful advocate of the aspirations of Third World countries within the United Nations. Using its numerical strength within the General Assembly, this group urged the United Nations to address many of the developmental issues that that body had neglected or slighted since its formation. Their focus, in terms of corporate multinationalism, was to work for international rules that would guarantee that these corporations would respect the "economic sovereignty" of the countries in which they invested.

From the perspective of Third World nations, so-called "developmental economics" involved much more than the unilateral infusion of capital, technology, and forceful management style into a backward economy. In Third World countries, developmental economics meant an investment policy that respected the "economic sovereignty" of the host countries. Not surprisingly, the established multinational corporations in developed countries were uncomfortable about the ultimate implications of this insistence on economic sovereignty. They soon realized, however, that it had become an inevitable component of all international investments in the Third World. Minimally speaking, it introduced a note of uncertainty if not apprehension into the corporate board rooms of U.S.-based firms as well as those of Europe and Japan.[26]

From another quarter came a further concern, namely, the expanding efforts of international trade unions to influence the policies of corporate multinationals on a global basis. American firms had never been particularly concerned about the agenda of international trade unions. Corporate America's casual attitude in the postwar years was traceable to the fact that the American labor movement, with the exception of the United Automobile Workers under Walter Ruther, had little interest in the policies of the international trade unions. What American multinational firms discovered during the '70s, however, was that these international unions had an agenda that represented a more serious and subtle threat to multinational enterprises than that posed by the American labor movement.

Many of the international unions sought to have a voice in management, to share in the decisions that affected the future of the company. And, unlike the American labor movement, they generally accepted corporate multinationalism as a given in the postwar world. They were multinational organizations themselves, and they were comfortable with multinationalization in the corporate world.

U.S.-based multinational firms, particularly those with sizeable facilities in the European Economic Community (EEC), discovered they had to deal with unions with more radical objectives than their American counterparts. For the moment, the economic and monetary dislocations within the world and the apparent invincibility of OPEC tempered the aggressiveness of the international trade union movement, but these unions had an ideological perspective that in the eyes of the American multinational corporation bore careful watching.[27]

It was becoming apparent that the corporate monitoring process and negative climate had gone international, forcing the Federal government and American multinational firms to adjust to a more amorphous set of ground rules and a more fluid power structure.

Reagan's landslide election to the presidency in 1980 was considered a virtual guarantee that at least the executive branch of government would promote a conservative economic policy. He had promised to reduce the presence of the Federal government in a broad range of activities, replacing it with a proclaimed "federalism" that would make the individual states and various private agencies the principal instruments of regulation or service that, up to this time, had been largely performed by agencies of the Federal government. His goals instinctively invited comparison with Herbert Hoover, and his management style suggested similarities with the Eisenhower administration.

Yet, by the '80s, the corporate community had become too politically sophisticated to take this historically comfortable perspective at face value. Even though most businessmen realized that as president Reagan was not going to be able to do everything he wanted to do, they knew there would be a more receptive climate in Washington, at least in the executive branch. To have Malcolm Baldridge in the Commerce Department, George Schultz in the State Department, and "Cap" Weinberger in the Defense Department was to have a coterie of businessmen drawn from the upper echelons of Fortune 500 companies in key cabinet posts. Regulatory agencies were certain to be less regulatory and environmentalists and advocates of an accident-free work place or minority rights were certain to be more "realistic" in their policies. Even Reagan's projected budget cuts were considered "prudent" given the economic and fiscal problems that had confronted the Ford and Carter administrations.

Midway through his administration (February, 1985), President Reagan reminded Congress that in his view:

The Federal Government has only a few important economic responsibilities. Given a proper conduct of these important roles, additional Federal intervention is more often a part of the problem than a part of the solution. We should continue to reduce the many less-important economic activities of the Federal Government so that individuals, private institutions, and State and local governments will have more resources and more freedom to pursue their own interests.[28]

It signaled his unflinching commitment to laissez-faire even though the administration knew it could never be implemented in its purest form.

If Washington was more benevolent toward corporate America, or at least perceived to be so, the world was not. The evidence was everywhere. No longer an occasional or isolated incident, corporate terrorism was on the rise, and it was international in scope and ruthless in implementation.[29] Everywhere there were politically explosive human rights issues that could not be ignored without damaging a company's image. Continued investments in South Africa for example, or new or expanded investments in South Korea or in the Philippines of Ferdinand Marcos were now considered image-damaging investments. Many of the more visible multinational corporations felt they could no longer afford to invest in a country when that country's government held power by force and insisted on adhering to policies that ignored basic human rights and abused its citizens. In effect, most multinational firms recognized they were being called upon to adopt policies that reflected not just profits, but the human rights values of enlightened world public opinion. They were expected to deny countries such as South Africa or South Korea the economic benefits of their presence.

But as the corporate community witnessed the laissez-faire years of the Reagan administration draw to a close, political and economic analysts began to refer more and more frequently to "global business" and to a "global economy." The terms had been used in the past, of course, but there was beginning to be a more deliberate use of the concept of global patterns, drifting away from the perspective that analyzed the international economy in terms of "world trading systems," an expression that implied multiple economies and a lack of cohesiveness, if not open rivalry. There was also a subtle shift in the perceived influence of the United States. Up to this time, America had a "role" to play in world trade—always, it should be noted, an important role—but now it seemed to be acquiring a "place" in the global economy. The differences were not merely semantic; they were substantive.[30]

And there was good reason for the change. With the collapse of Communist governments in Eastern Europe and the Soviet Union, and the apparent willingness of these countries to imitate the West and introduce, or at least try to introduce, market economies, there developed a heightened sensitivity to a truly global perspective when it came to considering broad economic issues. The Bush administration reflected this changing perspective and incorporated it into the President's first economic report to Congress. The February, 1990 report is replete with references to "global" patterns in the sections that review trading, fiscal, and monetary policies.[31]

This different perspective for economic policy analysis—more evident in the executive than in the legislative branch of government[32]—was paralleled by a different perspective in the corporate world, an awareness that there was a gradual transformation taking place in the structural configuration of many of the world's largest corporations. An increasing number of multinational corporations were transforming themselves into corporations that were more "global" than multinational.[33] Equally important was the development of what the Japanese were calling *keiretsu*—loosely structured combines that stressed integrating specific business functions on an *ad hoc* basis rather than altering the corporate structures of the participating companies.[34] Both developments, probably an outgrowth of the increased popularity of the joint venture phenomenon of the '70s, introduced a pattern of business activity that brought into question the continued appropriateness of the expression "American multinational corporation." What was obviously a valid expression to identify a powerful component of corporate America in the '50s, '60s, '70s, and even possibly the '80s, seemed to be losing its distinctiveness as it became increasingly difficult to identify the "home" country of many of the world's largest corporations.

To the extent that specialists began to analyze the phenomenon of the "stateless corporation" and examine the characteristics of the "global manager," they narrowed the meaning and historical significance of the concept, "American multinational corporation" and made it increasingly difficult to find a partnership relationship between these corporations and the U.S. government.

President Bush's efforts to open up Japan's markets to American products in January, 1992, headline-catching as it was because he chose to bring twenty-one corporate executives with him to improve his negotiating position, might well mask the reality of the corporate world as it seems to be evolving in the '90s. Technically speaking, some of the more powerful executives that accompanied President Bush to Japan were not the heads of American multinational corporations but were the CEOs of global or "stateless" corporations that really serve multiple national economic constituencies.

If it becomes increasingly difficult to identify the "nationality" of a corporation seemingly headquartered in the United States, then President Bush's trip to Japan might well be of considerable historic significance, highlighting as it does the problems associated with using prominent corporate executives of companies with multiple national economic constituencies to revitalize what is really only one of their economic constituencies—the United States.

It would appear that the visible and frequently censured postwar partnership between the Federal government and the "American" multinational corporation is beginning to fade.

NOTES

1. U.S. President, *Economic Report of the President Transmitted to the Congress, 1978* (Washington: G.P.O., 1978), pp. 1–237. Carter's letter of transmittal is 20 pages long and reflects the theme that there are still problems stemming from the recession of 1974–1975. The report itself refers to a "hesitant" recovery and has a chapter entitled "Inflation and Unemployment."

2. *Facts on File*, April 14, 1978, pp. 259–261; ibid., May 19, 1978, pp. 361–367.

3. *Congressional Quarterly Almanac, 1978*, p. 218 (henceforth cited as *CQA*).

4. Leonard Silk, "Economic Scene," [column], *New York Times*, June 15, 1978, Sec. 6, p. 2.

5. *Wall Street Journal*, July 21, 1978, p. 4 (emphasis added).

6. *New York Times*, June 26, 1978, pp. 1, D10.

7. See Neil H. Jacoby, Peter Nehemkis, and Richard Eells, "Foreign Payoffs Law: A Costly Error," ibid., Jan. 22, 1978, Sec. 3, p. 14.

8. *CQA, 1978*, pp. 267–269.

9. U.S. Congress, House, Committee on International Relations, Subcommittee on International Economic Policy and Trade, and the Subcommittee on International Development, Hearings before ..., *The Bonn Summit: Its Aftermath and New International Economic Initiatives* (Washington: G.P.O., 1978), pp. 1–111; and Robert D. Putnam and Nicholas Bayne, H*anging Together: The Seven-Power Summits* (London: Heinemann Press for the Royal Institute of International Affairs, 1984), pp. 100–115 [this material authored by N. Bayne].

10. Ibid.

11. Three U.N. studies issued in 1978, 1983, and 1988, respectively, chart the

evolution of the multinational corporation from the mid-'70s to the mid-'80s, placing the American multinational corporation in the context of world economic developments. U.N. Economic and Social Council, Commission on Transnational Corporations, *Transnational Corporations in World Development: A Re-Examination* (New York: United Nations, 1978) [there had been an earlier study in 1973]; *Transnational Corporations in World Development: Third Survey* (New York: United Nations, 1983); and *Transnational Corporations in World Development: Trends and Prospects* (New York: United Nations, 1988), (henceforth cited as *Transnational Corporations in World Development* [1978]; *Transnational Corporations in World Development* [1983]; and *Transnational Corporations in World Development* [1988]).

See also Robert G. Hawkins and Ingo Walker, "Multinational Corporations: Current Trends and Future Prospects," for U.S. Congress, Joint Economic Committee, in *Special Study on Economic Change, vol. 9, The International Economy: U.S. Role in a World Market, December 17, 1980* (Washington: G.P.O., 1980), pp. 686–736 (henceforth cited as *Special Study in Economic Change, vol. 9*).

12. *New York Times*, May 13, 1979, Sec. 6, p. 17.

13. See Raymond Vernon, "The Multinationalization of U.S. Business: Some Basic Policy Implications," in *Special Study in Economic Change, vol. 9*, pp, 737–747.

14. *CQA, 1978*, pp. 459–460.

15. *Wall Street Journal, Index, 1978; Wall Street Journal, Index, 1979*. See also *New York Times, Index, 1978*, p. 4, "Aerospace" entry.

16. *Wall Street Journal*, Aug. 2, 1979, pp. 1, 19; *Wall Street Journal*, "Murder in the Cathedral," [editorial], Dec. 27, 1979, p. 10; *New York Times*, May 29, 1979, Sec. 4, pp. 1, 6.

17. *New York Times*, May 29, 1979, Sec. 4, pp. 1, 6.

18. Ibid.; *Wall Street Journal*, Aug. 2, 1979, pp. 1, 19.

19. *New York Times*, June 12, 1979, Sec. 4, pp. 1, 15.

20. Ibid., June 17, 1979, Sec. 4, p. 5.

21. U.S. Congress, Senate, Judiciary Committee, Subcommittee on Antitrust, Monopoly, and Business Rights, Hearings before . . . , *Mergers and Economic Concentration*, Part 1, March 8 –April 25, 1979, Part 2, April 26–May 22, 1979 (Washington: G.P.O., 1979) and ibid., *Family Farm Antitrust Act of 1979*, May 15, July 17, Sept. 4, 1979 (Washington: G.P.O., 1979).

22. See *Economic Report of the President . . . , 1979* (Washington: G.P.O., 1979) and *Economic Report of the President . . . , 1980* (Washington: G.P.O., 1980).

It should be noted that the practice of issuing an annual *International Economic Report of the President* ceased in 1977 with the expiration of the International Economic Policy Act of 1972. Carter's last two general economic reports to Congress each had a chapter on the "World Economy." The 1979 report subtitled this chapter "Managing Interdependence," while the 1980 report subtitled its chapter "Testing Resilience." In neither chapter is there a reference to international business enterprises or multinational corporations as a force in, or as a victim of, the economic patterns discussed.

23. Seemingly, the first article in a major American magazine to suggest that the multinational corporation might not be the uncontrollable force that many feared

was a 1977 article in *Fortune* entitled "Why the Multinational Tide is Ebbing" by Stanford Rose (*Fortune*, August, 1977, pp. 111–120). Several years later a recognized critic of American multinational corporations, Richard J. Barnet, saw a loss of dominance by the multinational as one of the most significant characteristics of the late '70s, traceable, he maintained, to the policies of foreign governments and to the failure of American multinational corporations to secure consistent support from the American government (*The Lean Years, Politics in the Age of Scarcity* [New York: Simon and Schuster, 1980], pp. 239–244). From the perspective of 1986, *The Economist* published a major article: "American Multinationals Shrinking in the 1980's" supporting their thesis with impressive statistical data (*The Economist,* vol. 103, No. 7475, December 6, 1986).

24. This policy is most explicitly noted in the last *International Economic Report of the President Transmitted to Congress, 1977* (Washington: G.P.O., 1977), pp. 69–72. After 1977, opposition to the invasive policies that infringed on the investment strategies of the American multinational are briefly noted in the major U.N. studies cited below: *Transnational Corporations in World Development* [1978], pp. 25–26, 27; *Transnational Corporations in World Development* [1983], pp. 55, 77, 80, 91, 97, 100–101, 103; *Transnational Corporations in World Development* [1988], pp. 241–243.

25. *Transnational Corporations in World Development* [1978], pp. 4–14, 17, 25–26, 27; ibid., [1988], pp. 241–243, 331–359.

See also Joseph M. Grieco, "American Multinationals and International Order," in *Institutions for Projecting American Values Abroad*, III, ed. by Kenneth W. Thompson (Lanham, MD: University Press of America, 1983), pp. 7–13.

26. Robert Gilpin, *The Political Economy of International Relations* (Princeton: Princeton University Press, 1987), pp. 298–301. See also Stephen D. Krasner, *Structural Conflict: The Third World Against Global Liberalism* (Berkeley: University of California Press, 1985).

27. U.S. Congress, House, Committee on Banking, Currency, and Housing, Subcommittee on International Trade, Investment, and Monetary Policy, *International Investment Uncertainty*, report prepared by the staff of the subcommittee on . . . (Washington: G.P.O., 1977), pp. 53–57.

See also C. Fred Bergsten, Thomas Horst, and Theodore H. Moran, *American Multinationals and American Interests* (Washington, DC: The Brookings Institution, 1978), pp. 119–120.

28. *U.S. President Economic Report of the President . . . , 1985* (Washington: G.P.O., 1985), p. 9. This was the "Conclusion" in President Reagan's letter of transmittal that preceded the formal report.

29. *New York Times*, Feb. 19, 1978, Sec. F, p. 14; ibid., Nov. 19, 1979, Sec. 4, pp. 1, 6.

30. The economic reports of the President to Congress during the Carter and Reagan years more often than not referred to a "world trading system," "international capital markets," "world economy," and an "international economic system." These terms, perfectly valid concepts in international political economy, began to lose their generic dominance to such expressions as "global coordination," "global network," and organizing on a "global basis." They began to appear with greater frequency in President Bush's first economic report to Congress. He has a subsection

in his letter of transmittal entitled "The Global Economy" and a chapter in the report entitled "Growth and Market Reform in the Global Economy." *Economic Report of the President . . . ,* 1990 (Washington: G.P.O., 1990), pp. 7, 225–264.

31. Ibid.

32. During the Reagan years, Congress made technical adjustments in the largely dormant Foreign Corrupt Practices Act of 1977, authorized U.S. participation in the new Multilateral Investment Guarantee Agency, an affiliate of the World Bank, cleared legislation allowing OPIC to operate in China, and sporadically held hearings on issues or subjects with which American multinational corporations were tangentially involved.

33. Robert B. Reich, "Who is Us?" *Harvard Business Review,* vol. 68 (Jan.–Feb., 1990), pp. 53–64 and Professor Reich's companion piece, "Who is Them?" ibid., vol. 69 (March–April, 1991), pp. 77–88. See also "Economic Viewpoint," *Business Week,* Oct. 15, 1990 and "The Stateless Corporation," the cover story in ibid., May 14, 1990.

34. Ibid., Jan. 27, 1992.

SELECT BIBLIOGRAPHY

GENERAL

Annual Report. *Overseas Private Investment Corporation,* 1970/71–1990/91. Washington: OPIC, 1971–1991.

Congressional Quarterly Service. *Congressional Quarterly Almanac,* 1945–1991. Washington, DC: Congressional Quarterly, Inc., 1946–1992.

U.S. President. *Economic Report of the President Transmitted to Congress,* [annual] 1947–1991. Washington: G.P.O., 1947–1991.

_____. *International Economic Report of the President to Congress,* [annual] 1973–1977. Washington: G.P.O., 1973–1977.

_____, Commerce Department. *Survey of Current Business,* [annual] 1940–1991. Washington: G.P.O., 1940–1992.

STANDARD STUDIES OF AMERICAN MULTINATIONAL CORPORATIONS

Barnet, R. J. and Muller, R. E. *Global Reach: The Power of the Multinational Corporation.* New York: Simon & Schuster, 1974.

Bergsten, C. F., Horst, T., and Moran, T. H. *American Multinationals and American Interests.* Washington, DC: The Brookings Institution, 1978.

Hymer, S. H. *The International Operations of National Firms: A Study of Direct Foreign Investment.* Cambridge: MIT Press, 1976.

Vernon, R. *Sovereignty at Bay: The Multinational Spread of U.S. Enterprise.* New York: Basic Books, 1971.

_____. *Storm over the Multinationals: The Real Issues.* Cambridge: Harvard University Press, 1977.

Wilkins, M. *The Emergence of Multinational Enterprise: American Business Abroad from the Colonial Era to 1914.* Cambridge: Harvard University Press, 1970.

_____. *The Maturing of Multinational Enterprise: American Business Abroad from 1914 to 1970.* Cambridge: Harvard University Press, 1974.

BACKGROUND

Atwood, J. R. and Brewster, K. *Antitrust and American Business Abroad.* Colorado Springs, CO: Shephard's/ McGraw-Hill, 1981. 2 vols.

Binder, B. *International Labour Affairs: The World Trade Unions, and the Multinational Companies.* Oxford, England: The Clarendon Press, 1987.

Black, R., Blank, S., and Hanson, E. *Multinationals in Contention: Responses at Governmental and International Levels.* New York: The Conference Board, 1978.

Bork, R. H. *The Antitrust Paradox: A Policy at War with Itself.* New York: Basic Books, 1978.

Chandler, A. D., Jr. *The Visible Hand: The Managerial Revolution in American Business.* Cambridge: Harvard University Press, 1977.

Cochran, T. C. *American Business in the Twentieth Century.* Cambridge: Harvard University Press, 1972.

_____. *200 Years of American Business.* New York: Basic Books, 1977.

Epstein, E. M. *The Corporation in American Politics.* Englewood Cliffs, NJ: Prentice-Hall, Inc., 1969.

Flanagan, R. J. and Weber, A. R. *Bargaining Without Boundaries: The Multinational Corporation and International Labor Relations.* Chicago: University of Chicago Press, 1975.

Galambos, L. and Pratt, J. *The Rise of the Corporate Commonwealth: United States Business and Public Policy in the 20th Century.* New York: Basic Books, 1988.

Gilpin, R. *The Political Economy of International Relations.* Princeton: Princeton University Press, 1987.

Kaufman, B. J. *Trade and Aid: Eisenhower's Foreign Economic Policy, 1953–1961.* Baltimore: Johns Hopkins University Press, 1982.

Kujawa, D., ed. *American Labor and the Multinational Corporation.* New York: Praeger Publishers, 1973.

_____, ed. *International Labor and Multinational Enterprise.* New York: Praeger Publishers, 1975.

Mason, E. S., ed. *The Corporation in Modern Society.* Cambridge: Harvard University Press, 1959.

McQuaid, K. *Big Business and Presidential Power: From FDR to Reagan.* New York: William Morrow and Co., Inc., 1982.

Odell, J. S. *U.S. International Monetary Policy: Markets, Power and Ideas as a Source of Change.* Princeton: Princeton University Press, 1982.

Pastor, R. A. *Congress and the Politics of U.S. Foreign Economic Policy, 1929–1976.* Berkeley: University of California Press, 1980.

Robinson, J. *Multinationals and Political Control*. New York: St. Martin's Press, 1983.
Scammell, W. M. *The International Economy Since 1945*. 2nd ed. New York: St. Martin's Press, 1983.
Schriftgiesser, K. *Business and Public Policy, The Role of the Committee for Economic Development: 1942–1967*. Englewood Cliffs, NJ: Prentice-Hall, Inc., 1967.
Whitman, M. von Neumann. *Government Risk-Sharing in Foreign Investment*. Princeton: Princeton University Press, 1965.

GOVERNMENT STUDIES (EXECUTIVE BRANCH)

Peterson [Peter G.] Report. U.S. President. *The United States in a Changing World Economy*: vol. 1, *A Foreign Policy Perspective;* vol. 2, *Background Material*. Washington: G.P.O., 1972.
U.S. President, Commerce Department, Bureau of International Commerce. *The Multinational Corporation: Studies in U.S. Foreign Investment*. Washington: G.P.O., 1972–1973. Vol. 1 prepared by the Bureau of International Commerce; vol. 2 prepared by the Conference Board for the Secretary of Commerce.
———, Report of Commission on International Trade and Investment Policy. *United States International Economic Policy in an Interdependent World, Report of . . .*, I; *Papers of . . .*, II and III. Washington: G.P.O., 1971.
Watson [Arthur K.] Report, in David A. Baldwin, ed. *Foreign Aid and American Foreign Policy: A Documentary Analysis*. New York: Frederick A. Praeger, 1966.

CONGRESSIONAL HEARINGS AND STUDIES

U.S. Congress, House, Committee on Banking, Currency, and Housing, Subcommittee on International Trade, Investment, and Monetary Policy, report prepared by staff of subcommittee. . . . *International Investment Uncertainty*. Washington: G.P.O., 1977.
———, House, Committee on Foreign Affairs, hearings before. . . . *Role of Private Sector in Development Abroad*. Washington: G.P.O., 1982.
———, House, Committee on Foreign Affairs, study prepared for. . . . *The Overseas Private Investment Corporation: A Critical Analysis*. Washington: G.P.O., 1973.
———, House, Committee on Foreign Affairs, Subcommittee on Africa, hearings before. . . . *U.S. Business Involvement in Southern Africa,* Parts 1–3. Washington: G.P.O., 1971–1973.
———, House, Committee on Foreign Affairs, Subcommittee on Foreign Economic Policy, hearings before. . . . *The Overseas Private Investment Corporation, May 22–June 20, 1973*. Washington: G.P.O., 1973.
———, House, Committee on Foreign Affairs, Subcommittee on Foreign Economic Policy. *Report of. . . . The Overseas Private Investment Corporation, October 21, 1973*. Washington: G.P.O., 1973.
———, House, Committee on International Relations [formerly Committee on Foreign

Affairs], Subcommittee on International Policy, hearings before. . . . *Activities of American Multinational Corporations Abroad.* Washington: G.P.O., 1975.

_____, Joint Economic Committee. *Special Study on Economic Change,* vol. 9: *The International Economy: U.S. Role in a World Market, December 17, 1980.* Washington: G.P.O., 1981.

_____, Joint Economic Committee, Subcommittee on Foreign Economic Policy, hearings before. . . . *A Foreign Economic Policy for the 1970s,* Part 2: *Trade Policy Toward Developed Countries;* Part 4: *The Multinational Corporation and International Investment.* Washington: G.P.O., 1970.

_____, Senate, Committee on Banking, Housing, and Urban Affairs, hearings before. . . . *Foreign and Corporate Bribes.* Washington: G.P.O., 1976.

_____, Senate, Committee on Banking, Housing, and Urban Affairs, hearings before. . . . *Foreign Corrupt Practices and Domestic and Foreign Investment Disclosures.* Washington: G.P.O., 1977.

_____, Senate, Committee on Finance, Subcommittee on International Trade, hearings before. . . . *Foreign Trade, World Trade, and Investment Issues,* Part 1: *Hearings . . . ;* Part 2: *Appendixes.* Washington: G.P.O., 1971.

_____, Senate, Committee on Finance, Subcommittee on International Trade, hearings before. . . . *Multinational Corporations, February–March, 1973,* includes staff report of Committee on Finance, "The Multinational Corporation and the World Economy," and staff report of the AFL-CIO Maritime Trade Department, "Multinationals—The Dimming of America." Washington: G.P.O., 1973.

_____, Senate, Committee on Finance, Subcommittee on International Trade, papers solicited by. . . . *Multinational Corporations: A Compendium of Papers.* Washington: G.P.O., 1973.

_____, Senate, Committee on Finance, Subcommittee on International Trade, report prepared by the U.S. Tariff Commission for the Committee . . . , and Subcommittee. . . . *Implications of Multinational Firms for World Trade and Investment and for U.S. Trade and Labor.* Washington: G.P.O., 1973.

_____, Senate, Committee on Foreign Relations, Subcommittee on Multinational Corporations, hearings before. . . . *Multinational Corporations and United States Foreign Policy,* Part 1: *March 30–April 3, 1973;* Part 2: *Appendix to Part 1;* Part 3: *Overseas Private Investment Corporation;* Part 4–9: *Multinational Petroleum Companies and Foreign Policy;* Part 10: *Investments by Multinational Companies in Communist Bloc Countries;* Part 11: *Political and Financial Consequences of the OPEC Price Increase;* Part 12: *Political Contributions to Foreign Governments;* Part 13: *Multinational Corporations in the Dollar Devaluation Crisis;* Part 14: *Lockheed Aircraft Corporation;* Part 15: *Multinational Banks and U.S. Foreign Policy;* Part 16: *International Grain Companies;* Part 17: August 9– September 27, 1976. Washington: G.P.O., 1973–1977.

_____, Senate, Committee on Foreign Relations, Subcommittee on Multinational Corporations, report of subcommittee . . . to Committee on Foreign Relations. *Multinational Oil Corporations and U.S. Foreign Policy.* Washington: G.P.O., 1975.

_____, Senate, Committee on Foreign Relations, Subcommittee on Multinational Corporations, study requested by. . . . *Direct Investment Abroad and the Multinational: Effects on the United States Economy,* by Peggy B. Musgrave. Washington: G.P.O., 1973.

MAJOR SERIAL PUBLICATIONS OF CORPORATE INTEREST GROUPS

Business International. *Business International*. [1957–1990].
Business Roundtable. *Roundtable Report*. [1980–Present].
Conference Board. *Record*. [1946–1976] and *Across the Board* [1976–Present].

GUIDES FOR U.S. CORPORATIONS ENGAGED IN INTERNATIONAL BUSINESS

Delphos, William A., ed. *Washington's Best Kept Secrets: A U.S. Government Guide to International Business*. New York: John Wiley, 1983.
SEC. *Questionable and Illegal Corporate Payments and Practices*. Washington: G.P.O., 1976.
U.S. President, Department of Justice, Antitrust Division. *Antitrust Guide for International Operations*. Washington: G.P.O., 1977.

UNITED NATIONS PUBLICATIONS ON MULTINATIONAL CORPORATIONS

United Nations, Department of Economic and Social Affairs, Center on Multinational Corporations. *Multinational Corporations in World Development*. New York: United Nations, 1973.
_____, Economic and Social Council, Commission on Transnational Corporations. *Transnational Corporations in World Development: A Re-Examination*. New York: United Nations, 1978.
_____, Economic and Social Council, Commission on Transnational Corporations. *Transnational Corporations in World Development: Third Survey*. New York: United Nations, 1983.
_____, Economic and Social Council, Commission on Transnational Corporations. *Transnational Corporations in World Development: Trends and Prospects*. New York: United Nations, 1988.
_____, *Summary of Hearings Before The Group of Eminent Persons to Study the Impact of Multinational Corporations on Development and International Relations*. New York: United Nations, 1974.

SPECIAL STUDIES

Gaston, J. F. *Obstacles to Direct Foreign Investment: Report Prepared for the President's Committee for Financing Foreign Trade*. New York: National Industrial Conference Board, 1951.
Interfaith Center on Corporate Responsibility. *Agribusiness Manual: Background Papers on Corporate Responsibility and Hunger Issues*. New York: Interfaith Center on Corporate Responsibility, 1978.
Jacoby, N. H., Nehemkis, P., and Eells, R. *Bribery and Extortion in World Business; A*

Study of Corporate Political Payments Abroad. New York: Macmillan & Co.,
    1977.
U.S. Department of Commerce. *Business Council: A Review of its Activities Since its
    Original Formation* . . . [in] June, 1933. n.p., n.d.

INDEX

About the Author

JOHN J. REARDON is Professor of History at Loyola University in Chicago. He is the author of *Edmond Randolph: A Biography* (1974) and *Peyton Randolph, 1721–1775: One Who Presided* (1982).